The Beginning
From Opportunity Comes Unlimited Success

UNLIKELY DESTINY

VOLUME ONE

Joe E. Pryor Jr.

BALBOA
PRESS
A DIVISION OF HAY HOUSE

Balboa Press books may be ordered through booksellers or by contacting:

Balboa Press
A Division of Hay House
1663 Liberty Drive
Bloomington, IN 47403
www.balboapress.com
1 (877) 407-4847

Because of the dynamic nature of the Internet, any web addresses or links contained in this book may have changed since publication and may no longer be valid. The views expressed in this work are solely those of the author and do not necessarily reflect the views of the publisher, and the publisher hereby disclaims any responsibility for them.

The author of this book does not dispense medical advice or prescribe the use of any technique as a form of treatment for physical, emotional, or medical problems without the advice of a physician, either directly or indirectly. The intent of the author is only to offer information of a general nature to help you in your quest for emotional and spiritual well-being. In the event you use any of the information in this book for yourself, which is your constitutional right, the author and the publisher assume no responsibility for your actions.

Any people depicted in stock imagery provided by Getty Images are models, and such images are being used for illustrative purposes only.
Certain stock imagery © Getty Images.

Print information available on the last page.

ISBN: 978-1-9822-0052-7 (sc)
ISBN: 978-1-9822-0054-1 (hc)
ISBN: 978-1-9822-0053-4 (e)

Library of Congress Control Number: 2018903613

Balboa Press rev. date: 04/11/2018

Thank you, Jessica for believing in me…

CONTENTS

FOREWORD

My friend Joe opens his insightful book with a tense scene. Undergoing surgery after a traffic collision in his police car, Joe's blood pressure skyrocketed and caused his heart to stop for 45 seconds. Following this near-death experience, Joe woke up with a lot of questions. "Am I a good person, father, son, friend, teacher, and listener" he asked. "Am I being honest with myself about the life I'm living?"

There's often a moment in life that prompts us to ask the big, difficult questions. Mine was in 1999. I was at the top of my game, host of a TV show, feeling invincible, when my doctor told me that I had Multiple Sclerosis. He said I'd be in a wheelchair in four years and dead in 10. It felt like that moment when you reach the top of a hill, convinced that the challenging part is behind you, only to spot an impossible mountain on the other side. After my diagnosis, I asked myself: "Why me?" and "Why can't someone fix this?" But those were the wrong questions, I realized. I decided I could spend the rest of my life feeling sorry for myself, or start asking the right questions. What can I learn about my illness? How can I use that knowledge to help others? How do I become a better person and father?

Drawing from his experience as a police officer, husband, father, and writer, Joe—with his characteristic wisdom, sensitivity, and keen insight— tackles the big questions that confront every one of us. How do you achieve a big dream? Joe writes about growing up in a lower middle-class home in Watts and Compton during the 1960's and 1970's. It was a tough time to be a young black man in America (I'll vouch for that) and, often, you'd feel as if having dreams was a luxury reserved for other people. But as Joe writes—and demonstrates—if you seize opportunities and work hard at them, no dream is out of reach. But how late is too late? Sometimes, in reflecting on a dream, we'll tell ourselves, "That ship has sailed." But as Joe writes: "You should see a multitude of new beginnings." Indeed, every morning is a new opportunity to take that first step toward achieving a goal, or becoming the person you wish to be. So how do you take that first step? You trust yourself. You acknowledge there will be obstacles, but trust you're equipped with the courage and character to tackle them. Joe describes writing his book as an example. The task felt daunting at first, but by trusting his vision, he found the courage to type those first words. How do you overcome the obstacles? Joe recommends positive thinking and "an environment full of positive, focused and motivated people." I agree there's no better recipe. After my diagnosis with MS, I surrounded myself with positive people who encouraged, challenged, and inspired me to get better and become better. It's why I'm grateful to call Joe a friend and find inspiration in his words, on and off the page.

Montel Williams

PREFACE

WHAT IS THE UNIVERSE TRYING TO TELL YOU?

When I began the process of writing Unlikely Destiny, I knew for many years that I wanted to write something. A book, a stage play, or maybe a screenplay, possibly a short film. I wanted to do something in the creative arts, but what would it be? I took a long honest look at my life one day and I realized writing a book or books, is what I wanted to do! Now I tested the waters in every area of the above listed possibilities and decided I wanted to write books that would help people see, accept and fully understand, their life's true purpose and potential, but most of all their destiny!

When I ask the question, "What Is The Universe Trying To Tell You?" I want you to take a real and honest look at your life, without all of the everyday drama and unfortunate circumstances that you are currently living and put your life into perspective. I want you to see the circumstances you have adopted and learn how to change your environment by first, "Wanting to change that environment." Now when I talk about "ENVIRONMENT," I'm not just talking about a location or where you may live. Our environment encompasses the individual, (YOU) along with everyone we accept and invite in. Did you know you could become the sum total of the environment you create? Knowing that, I would say be careful about what you are building and who is helping you in this build.

"Focus Forward", is the mindset I go to sleep with and wake up with, all day every day. Always moving forward with a positive attitude and a belief that I can do anything I put my mind to, is my new normal. I also realized one day, it's okay to be happy. Happy is good place to live!

What Is The Universe Trying To Tell You? I fought with the Universe for years, wanting to write, but not really believing I could. I avoided the idea of writing and lived in denial about it for too many years. Who was I to write anything I thought? Meanwhile the job I held for twenty plus years as a police officer, was that of a "True Life" story teller. A police report is the real-life account of, in many cases, an unfortunate situation that has been told to you by the victim or a witness, of a crime. Being able to translate a victim's detailed information into a police report, is what was needed to get a conviction and secure the arrest of a suspect. I was a writer!!! The thought of writing a book still scared the hell out of me, but I was doing it every day. "On The Job Life Training," is what I like to call it. Something you may be doing every day or the environment you live your life in, could be preparing you for your true life's work, your Destiny! Writing was always my passion and it ran deep in my spirit. My PDD, or Passion, Drive and Desire came in the form of putting pen to paper, to document the thoughts that lived inside my spirit, and using my life's experiences for two things: First, doing what I loved "WRITING" and Second, using my first love to, "HELP" everyone around me live up to their true and full potential! "WE", are in many cases here to do more, than what we wake up and do, or not do every day! Each and every one of us are given special talents, gifts, or abilities and the most unfortunate aspect of having these gifts is, not recognizing we have them. In some cases, we have them, but don't know how or when to use them. Unlikely Destiny, is just what it says... It is Unlikely because it's right in front of you, in some manner, fashion or form, you just can't see it! Sometimes "DESTINY" is lost due to mindset, or timing and in many cases not believing in ourselves enough to succeed, but nevertheless it's there. This could be why we don't see it! I thank God every day for allowing me to see and understand my destiny. I believe it was a gift placed clearly in front of me to be opened and used. Unlikely Destiny, is understanding your spirit holds the key to your destiny, through the dreams that are embedded in your DNA from the day you are born, just waiting to be unleashed. If you would learn to stop, look and listen: STOP, living your life for everyone else, LOOK, at everything, every day, that is being gifted to you to help you fulfill your destiny and LISTEN, to everyone you meet good, bad or otherwise, because this information has been created to help you, on your journey to SUCCESS!

The main thought I had while writing Unlikely Destiny, was to open your eyes and assist your steps, Focus Forward to Enlightenment, through Thought, Self-Awareness, and a Belief in Possibility? I want you to question yourself about the effort you put into living your life? I want you to ask yourself every day, "WHY NOT ME?" Like I said before, many of us are born to do more than we think we can. When things happen outside of what we think are the normal parameters of who we believe we are, we are at times unaware that our true destiny could be within reach. There's a quote that says "Reach for the moon and if you don't make it at least you'll be amongst the stars!" My wish is that you wake up every day with a purpose, live your life Focus Forward and love your life like you mean it, and it means something!!!

INSPIRATION

My Inspiration while writing "Unlikely Destiny" was everyone who didn't believe in me and the blessings of every single person who did believed in me, and encouraged me, to never give up on anything!!! My Inspiration is also a constant reminder that no matter how successful you become, you cannot and will not do anything alone! To My mother Hattie Moore who gave birth to me and put a fire in my spirit that will never burn out. My father Joe E. Pryor Sr. and my step-mother Josephine Pryor, my grandmother's Pinkie Thomas and Susan Littlejohn who gave me a foundation that allowed me to stand firmly on my own two feet. My father also taught me that my name had to mean something to "ME" above and beyond a signature on a piece of paper. Respect, Honor, Passion, Drive and Desire became the strength behind my name and everything it represents. My sixth-grade elementary school teacher, Laura Hamm, from 96th Street Elementary, gave me hope for a positive future by not allowing me, or any of my classmates to feel sorry for being Black. Foshay Jr. High School is where I would meet several teachers that would help me make the decision to truly become an individual. I learned to be a leader and not a follower! Manual Arts High School, class of 78, (Ke Aliians, THE ROYAL ONES) is where I would meet one of the biggest influences in my life, Coach Reggie Morris! Coach Morris' influence made me want to become a better person, thereby creating a better man, who should always be responsible for his own actions. He was my basketball coach, who would become my first life coach. Life, like basketball is all about team. Coach Morris dealt with us as individuals, but in the process made us into a team. He taught me that there will be things you have to do alone, but in order to make it and become successful, you need to be a part of a team and learn to trust the process. When I arrived at Cal-State L.A. my Criminal Justice 101 instructor, Thel Glasscock said something to me one day that changed my life. He said, "College does not promise you a good job, but you will get an education if you apply yourself." Professor Glasscock also said, "You have to be happy in whatever you decide to do as a career." Since I've always had an entrepreneur's heart I left college after my third year and began a career in law enforcement. While I was in the Sheriff's Academy I met my next life coach, Sr. Deputy Jim Mahone, "The Ramrod" of Academy Class 210. Sr. Deputy Mahone, like Coach Morris, told us we have to be responsible for our action, but Sr. Deputy Mahone also told me, "My actions in the jail and on the streets would keep me alive or get me killed!" One of the first rules in officer safety is, "Respecting everyone the way you would respect yourself." This was true life and death advice for me.

Everyone we meet on our journey is placed on our path, good, bad or otherwise to help us! My next life coach would be Darlene Hayes, a multiple Emmy Award Winning Television Producer, Executive Producer and Writer, who would open my eyes to the world of writing. I had a desire to write and she fueled that desire with encouragement and guidance that put me on the path I'm on today. Darlene saw something in me before I realized it was there. Darlene was always positive and hard-working, but most of all she taught me to never be denied. Darlene introduced me to my next life coach, Montel Williams. Montel started as a client, became a friend, and grew into a mentor. Working with Montel over the past twenty-five years allowed me to be present during his motivational speaking engagements and the writing of every one of his New York Times Bestselling books. His guidance in my personal and professional life has afforded me a wealth of knowledge that I could not have received anywhere else. This was true on the job life training! One day I had an epiphany about what I wanted to do with my life... "Writer, Speaker and doing what I do best, Listener." Jim Rohn said, "You are the sum total of the five people you spend the most time with." I have to believe everyone I've met was placed in my life for a specific reason and I have been so blessed to have had these people play a significant role in my development and my character. As I look back, there are so many people that have given me advice and stood by my side through thick and thin. I am honored and always inspired, to call each and every one of them my friend.

INTRODUCTION

As I open the door to a new path in the history that is my life,
I take joy in this new adventure seeing what my life can be,
not forgetting what it was, while believing I can...

Joe E. Pryor Jr.

LIFEWORK JOURNAL ENTRY

It's February 1993, early morning...

I am currently a police officer for the Inglewood Police Department and it's several months after the L.A. "Rodney King" riots. My partner and I are involved in the pursuit of a vehicle that we would later find out was stolen during these same riots. We are traveling westbound on Century Blvd approaching The Los Angeles International Airport, and just before LaCienega Blvd my partner lost control of our vehicle and crashed. During the crash my left shoulder's rotator cuff was ripped out of its socket creating the most excruciating pain known to man!

I'm lying on a surgical gurney in an operating room, at Daniel Freeman Memorial Hospital, in Inglewood, California. It's a little after eight a.m. and I've been here since six in the morning, finally prepped for reconstructive surgery on my left rotator cuff. Today, will truly become the first day of the rest of my life. I have the opportunity now to think about the people in my life. Am I a good person, father, son, friend, teacher, and listener to these people? The people I love, have I told them "I love you" enough? Have I done enough in every situation to help everyone I could? Am I being honest with myself about the life I'm living? We don't often get second chances, or a, "Do Over" in life, but if we are so blessed to, we should make every second, of every day count because, it could be our last. Awake and coherent several things happened during my surgery, and I am happy and grateful to be here to talk about it.

The anesthesiologist had me start counting backwards from one hundred...

An extremely warm sensation took over my body just before I drifted off to sleep. Now, time feels as if it's standing still. I can hear voices in the distance, but I can't clearly understand what they are saying. The voices are somewhat muffled and I feel as if I am drifting further and further away from the operating room. They didn't sound too excited, but I did feel a sense of urgency in one of the male voices, which sounded like my surgeon. The voices slowly faded away and now I'm lying there in complete darkness and silence. My body is no longer cold like before, nor was it hot or warm, the way I felt just before going under the anesthesia. I was just there, and it was quiet. It was the kind of quiet you experience when you wake up at three in the morning and most of the world is still asleep. If you grew up or ever lived in California and happened to be awake during an earthquake, it's that kind of silence. Birds stop chirping; dogs and cats have an inner fear that drives them to want to run and hide. They can anticipate the shifting of the earth, so they find a quiet place to ride out their fear. That's where I am right now, but surprisingly I am not fearful. Am I still lying on the gurney in the operating room? I'm trying to understand how I am awake, but not feeling anything? During this period of silence, the dark void surrounding me has become extremely comforting. There is no fear, no anxiety, and no feelings of sadness or despair. I'm not sure where I am? I don't know if my eyes are open or closed because of the darkness, but the darkness surrounding me is filled with energy. This energy made me feel as if I were floating, so I'm not sure if I am still in the operating room or floating somewhere in space. Weightlessness comes to mind. It may not make any sense, but the only other way to explain it is being able to, "ONLY FEEL MY SPIRIT." My spirit feels more alive at this point than my physical body ever did! When people talk about feeling a joy in their hearts, my spirit is feeling the joy of a thousand hearts. (JOY is defined as, the emotion of great delight or happiness caused by something exceptionally good or satisfying; keen pleasure; elation.) This state gives me a sense of strength and power. I feel as if nothing can harm me. Fear, rejection, and negativity have no place here. At one point I began feeling like pure energy, but in its most simple form. (The total energy contained in an object is identified with its mass. Energy can't be created or destroyed.) If you've ever heard the phrases "good energy" or "bad energy," this energy feels good in every way imaginable. Think about some of the people you know: family, friends, co-workers, employees, etc. Some of these people can take every ounce of energy or spirit out of a room and out of you. They can change your mood and your attitude, sometimes causing you to make bad life decisions. There is a saying that goes, "misery loves company" and misery will pull you under if you don't fight it. Then there are those who can fill the same room with their spirit and "GOOD" energy bringing the world back to a better place for everyone they meet. I'm in that better place, and content to stay here! Even though I'm surrounded by this energy, the darkness I am resting in, is beginning to take over me and I'm becoming a part of the darkness. Again, this darkness I'm in does not feel evil or negative, it is just void of any light. From basic physics, in respects to energy, I know it cannot be created or destroyed. It can only be converted from one type to another. Energy was here before us, and it'll be here long after we are physically gone. I believe my physical body is becoming energy and my once physical being is becoming the darkness that surrounds me. I'm becoming a different type of energy, no longer flesh and bones or an intellectual being. I am becoming spirit.

I'm finally able to open my eyes, my head is positioned so that when my eyes open I'm looking down at my right hand. Another hand comes into view reaching for mine. As I look up I see my father. There is complete silence for what seems like forever and he appeared to be moving in slow motion. He continues looking at me with his warm but confident smile. My father has always been a no-nonsense person and a man of few words, but when he said something I made it a point to listen. Still holding my hand, he lifts it up, taking his eyes off mine for a second, he looks at our hands. Then he looks me in the eye and says… "Welcome back", but before I have an opportunity to answer him everything goes completely silent and I'm surrounded by that dark energy once again.

I'm in recovery coming out of an anesthesia fog. The room is spinning ever so slowly finally coming to a complete stop. My vision's clearing and coming into FOCUS. I see a nurse at the foot of my bed speaking to my anesthesiologist, who notices I am awake. He asked me several questions, but specifically how I was feeling. "I'm a little fuzzy in the head, my throat is extremely sore and there isn't any feeling in my left arm," I replied. "Your head and throat will clear, and the lack of pain or any feeling in your left arm is normal. You should be happy you're not feeling any pain yet." We both laughed as the nurse began checking my vitals. Noticeably my blood pressure is still extremely higher than it should be (145 over 105). My surgeon walked into the room and shook my hand. He advised me that the surgery on my left shoulder was a success, but there were some complications during the procedure, mainly the stoppage of my heart and then the issue with my blood pressure. He said that my blood pressure increased to an extremely fatal level causing my heart to go into tachycardia and stop for 45 seconds. He assured me that there was no loss of oxygen to my brain, and I did not suffer any permanent damage. Sometimes I beg to differ! As I continued to lie there not saying a word, after several seconds, I asked my doctor if I was okay. He reiterated, there were no problems, but they were going to keep me for observation due to the tachycardia, and they needed to get my blood pressure under control before they could safely release me. As he was giving me the last bit of information, my mom walked into the room. She had the most amazing smile on her face when she walked in, and I was so happy to see her! She held my right hand and gave me a kiss on my forehead, as I often did to her. We both smiled and she asked me how I was feeling. "I'm a little nervous mom, but I'll be fine." I said. "Has the doctor spoken to you about the tachycardia, and your heart stopping due to the high blood pressure?" she asked. "That's what we were talking about when you walked in," I told her. "He also advised me they were keeping me in the hospital for a day or two so they could monitor my heart and get my blood pressure under control." I'm still trying to figure out what happened to me during those forty-five seconds that my heart stopped. Clearly, I did not understand the magnitude of what happened to me, but in time I would.

"Mom, could you ask Dad to come in? I would like to talk to him." "He is running an errand, but should be back soon." she said. "Did he come into recovery to see me?" "No, I'm the first person they let in so far, but there are several guys from the station and a couple of your other friends in the waiting room." I was happy to hear about my co-workers and friends, but I was still taken back about the fact that my Dad never physically came into the recovery room. Not saying anything to my mom about what happened, I decided to wait to speak with my Dad about it. As my visitors came in to see me it was great to have them visit, but mentally I'm still in an extremely dark, and quiet place. I can hear every one around me talking, but I'm so far removed from everything. By the time my Dad returned to the hospital, they had put me in my own room and my head was clear of the anesthesia. Now my mom already told me my Dad had not come into recovery before her, but I had to ask him anyway. "Hey Dad, did you come into the recovery area to see and talk with me before now?" He replied, "No, this is the first time I'm seeing you since this morning, before the surgery." "Why?' he asked. I told him that I saw him standing near my bed, holding my hand, and welcoming me back. I told him that I thought he did this in the recovery room. His look alone answered my question. Now I know this vision happened during the time that my heart stopped. We had a discussion about what I believed to be my out of body experience, and he made it clear to me that he didn't have any knowledge of welcoming me back, physically, or spiritually. My father believes in God, and he is not doubting or discounting the fact that my out of body experience did or didn't happen. The way he summed it up was to say, "If you are still here, you must have work to do!" I decided right there, to never, ever waste another day, hour, minute, or second. Clearly, I'm still needed here, but I thought to myself, "what is it I'm supposed to do?" My father grabbed my right hand, similar to what happened in my vision, and began to pray for me. After he walked out of the room everything hit me like a ton of bricks. I cried like a baby, for the next thirty minutes. My tears were tears of confusion and sadness, but I am alive. I am alive. Finally realizing I have so much more to do with my life, my tears would eventually turn to joy.

Home for about a week now, I've done a lot of soul searching so to speak. The whole forty-five seconds of death thing is stuck in my spirit. Forty-five seconds! "Why not an entire minute?" I asked myself. This is going to be on my mind every minute, of every day, for the rest of my life. Looking back on my childhood, growing up in Watts and Compton, California, several of my friends and acquaintances, because of their actions, or possibly being in the wrong place at the wrong time made their way to prison, or even worse, the cemetery. I'm still here so that has allowed me a second, third, and fourth chance to live my life. What does my life mean? Today I live my life fifteen seconds at a time. Not literally, but living every second of my life with a belief in purpose that we are all here to help each other. Believing things happen in your life the way they are supposed to, keeps me on track. There is still a lot of work here for me to do. I've been given several gifts, but the most important gift I have is my life!

We are all here on our own journey trying to make our way through this life the best way we know how. Often times many of the people you meet, including family and friends, won't understand your journey. They won't understand your passion or your drive to do what it is you know you have to do. That's okay keep your Focus Forward because the only person who can stop you at this point is you! Enlightenment can bring about change. Change can open hearts. Open hearts can lift spirits and a lifted spirit can change the world. Living my life Focus Forward allows me to believe that any and everything is possible, and a negative past does not define or predict your future. You have to try and when you try, you have to believe that you can! I chose to start Unlikely Destiny Volume One, Chapter One, as The End and I will end Unlikely Destiny Volume One, Chapter Ten, as The New Beginning. Once you finish reading Unlikely Destiny Volume One, I hope that you understand the end of this book will be the beginning of you recognizing your Unlikely Destiny!

END LIFEWORK JOURNAL ENTRY

The End

WHAT DESTINY MEANS TO ME...

Follow your interest, get the best available education and training, set your sights high, be persistent, be flexible, keep your options open, accept help when offered and be prepared to help others.

Mildred Spiewak Dresselhaus

It was a morning quite like every morning of my life... I wake up; roll out of bed and on my knees, I pray. The only difference about this morning is, it's my fiftieth birthday. I'm a half-century old and as a child I never thought I'd make it this far. God has blessed me with another great year and I also give thanks for great family and friends. As I think about this fiftieth year, reflecting on my childhood: the good times, the hard times and specifically the bad times; thinking about all the crap I went through as a child I'm able to laugh at some of it. Some of it was just a little too serious to let go of and sits in my box, so learning to "DEAL" became a way to survive. Even though I've had hard times and some bad times, I'm still able to smile. "Never give up," became the mantra I learned to live my life by. By adopting a "never give up" attitude I came to believe, "From Opportunity Comes Unlimited Success." Every opportunity placed before me, I've taken advantage of them, but ultimately my survival became key.

LIFEWORK JOURNAL ENTRY

I don't quite remember how old I was, 3 or possibly 4, but I do remember waking up in the middle of the night, with what I believed to be, two very strong hands around my neck, choking the life out of me. I was so afraid I pissed all over my bed and myself. My eyes still closed, I was truly afraid to open them, because I didn't want to see, who or what was choking the life out of me! When I finally summoned the courage to open my eyes, I realized there was no one choking me. Was I dreaming? To a point I was dreaming, because there wasn't anyone physically choking me, but I was choking and I had truly pissed myself. First of all, I was a small child and I was unable to breathe. Each time I took a breath, I felt as though each one was going to be my last. I thought I was dying. I got out of my bed and made my way down the hallway of the apartment we lived in, to my parent's bedroom. I knocked on their bedroom door and even though I was unable to breathe, struggling for every breath, I was more afraid of what was going to happen to me for wetting my bed. I remember my parents being afraid when they saw me not being able to breathe and rushed me to the hospital. Looking back, this is the first of many struggles I had to learn to deal with. I was born with asthma, but I never had an attack so severe. Asthma was not a fun way to start your life, but these were the cards I was dealt, so I learned to deal. For the first thirteen years of my life, my lungs were plagued with difficulty exhaling, so when I had what was known as an Asthma Attack, I couldn't even blow out a candle if it was one inch from my mouth. If we allow circumstances to control our lives, those particular circumstances could give us every excuse to fail and in most cases without even knowing we did it. I was born with the perfect excuse to fail or just give up. I could have said, because I was a black male who grew up in the ghettos of Watts and Compton California, during some extremely tough times, what kind of future did I have? I could also say because my parents weren't rich, what chance did I have to make something out of my life? Joining a gang was another option. Again, I could have used every excuse in and out of the book, but I chose not to give up. Deep in my spirit, I always believed circumstances can and will change. Taking advantage of opportunities became a way to believe I could move ahead in life.

END LIFEWORK JOURNAL ENTRY

These opportunities, I later discovered, had been placed before me for a reason. They were always mine, but I didn't know it, or was not able to see them at the time because of a lack of clarity. If you look deep into your memories, you will discover there have been endless advantages presented to you in your life. I had heard for years, "Things happen for a reason." Being the child, I was, I always wondered what that phrase really meant. Everyone always associated this phrase with the negative things in our lives. Someone got shot or the Smith's car was stolen. Why was it that people never said this when positive things happened? Kenny graduated college or Shelia was able to get a home loan. How come we never associated good things with what we thought was fate? As I grew up I came to my own understanding about the way things happen in our lives. I believe things happened in your life the way they are supposed to. Choosing your path, whether consciously or unconsciously, every door you choose to open on your journey will determine your success or lack thereof. When these things do happen, good or bad, you have to be ready, willing and able to deal with them. When you have a better understanding of what's happening, this will also help to direct your steps to success. Now think about why things happen for you. The main reason I didn't allow myself to live a down and out defeated life is because of my parents. Now my parents were not easy on me growing up, but I believe it helped to prepare and develop me into the person I am today. If they didn't stay on me, I could have strayed in the wrong direction, down the wrong path, or maybe even wound up dead. That's just how things were. Another fact of life my parents pointed out to me was, "To take advantage of every opportunity placed before you." Taking advantage of those opportunities meant getting the education and the knowledge wherever, and whenever, I could. My mother would tell me, "It didn't cost anything to go to the library." I followed her advice and spent some of my spare time at the local library, reading everything I could to learn more about the world I lived in. Learning about life beyond my neighborhood gave me a desire to see the "Whole World" and I began realizing I was a part of it. My dad was old school and he believed, a man was his name and he always said to me, "Your name (meaning your last name) is all you have in this world. You're born with it, you're responsible for it and you'll die with it, so you have to respect it." Growing up, I came to understand what he meant (Self

Respect). If you don't respect you, who will he said? And when people see that you respect yourself, they are less likely to try and take advantage of you or disrespect you. He also said, "When you believe in you, others will do the same." One day I finally understood what my dad was saying about my name and talk about pressure! Having self-respect or respect for a name is not easy to understand as a child. As a child or even as an adult it's a lot better hearing your name being called when you've done something positive as opposed to negative. Your family's name is not just a name, it's your legacy. With that legacy, if you're smart, you develop a sense of honor. Whatever you do and wherever you go, so does your name. I realized it helped me to really keep myself in check so I didn't embarrass my family name. You see every time I did something in my neighborhood, good or bad I was known as, "Joe Pryor's son." Not just Joe, but Joe Pryor. It was sort of a checks and balances system I grew up with. You learned everything you did, good or bad would get back to your parents and the bad was never a good thing. As I got older everyone pretty much always called me by my first and last name. Introducing myself as, "Joe Pryor" became a habit I will never change. I'm not saying things are always going to be easy, because you're going to go through some crap from time to time. How you dealt with these situations would determine where you would come out in the wash, so to speak. Because so much crap happened to me as a child I had to create a positive acronym for the word "CRAP". So, for me "CRAAP" became, "Creating Real And Active Possibilities". This form of CRAAP kept everything moving in a positive Focus Forward direction. I've learned over my fifty plus years, everyone has grown up with one or more challenges in their life. For most of us life was not easy, but we don't give up. I'm just laying some of the groundwork for what I believe created the base of my Focus Forward foundation and my positive mindset was created, by learning to turn "CRAP" into "CRAAP."

The reality I created may not have been real but it was mine. I began learning how to FOCUS on getting my life in order. It took a little while, but I learned to call difficult times in my life "CHALLENGES." One day, I looked up the word "challenge" in my Webster's Dictionary. "Challenge" is a verb, giving several definitions. The first part of the definition that applies to my life is: "TO QUESTION THE TRUTH OF." Looking at this definition caused me to realize, all my life I've had questions about everything. Also, by asking questions, I became a reservoir of knowledge. I guess it was all the time I spent in the library opening up my mind. Learning is key in the forward progression of our lives. The second part of the definition: "TO ORDER TO HALT AND BE IDENTIFIED." So many times, in our lives, we have to take a step back. Stop, look and listen so you can clearly see, identify and understand the challenges you are faced with. They're not all going to be easy, but as you develop strength of mind, nothing will be able to stop you. Making situations in your life a challenge causes you to compete. We all need some form of competition. It's a healthy way to live and it's an extremely healthy way to learn. Think about growing up… all of your life, learning has come through some sort of challenge, or competition. Whether you're rich or poor challenges help to shape the people we've become. In many cases it starts at home as we begin competing with siblings. This is one of the first phases. If you're an only child when you get older and start going to school, even pre-school, we compete with our peers. As a natural course of our development competition will always create challenges. As you move forward in your education pretty much everything you do becomes a competition, i.e.: for grades, even for the attention of the opposite sex. Taking tests and competing for grades is another phase of competition. Sports create yet another type of competition or challenge, but it's still the challenge pulling us in.

Another challenge I faced as a kid, was growing up in Watts and Compton, California. I was born on June 7, 1960 at 12:26 AM and this could explain why I like being awake at night. Growing up in and around these two cities in the Sixties and Seventies was truly a challenge. It was during the time of the Non-Violent demonstrations, of Dr. Martin Luther King and the Civil Rights Movement. Malcolm X, with his "by any means necessary" motto is how I started and ended most of my days. Black Power and total power to the people was all around me. The Black Panther Movement was another staple in our community. They started out great, helping in the community by creating educational and food programs. They also became an extra set of eyes and ears in the black community keeping a watchful eye, on one or two bad apples of the local police. The Panthers also kept the local neighborhood riff raff in check. They truly became local heroes, especially to the young Black men in my neighborhood. It helped to keep the community strong and it also began to make Blacks proud of their neighborhoods. As time went on, one day according to government sources, they decided to overthrow the American government. Also, according to government sources, The Black Panther Party decided to incorporate a type of "Democratic Socialism." This democratic socialism indicates that, "the means of production are owned by the entire population and political power would be in the hands of the people democratically, through a co-operative commonwealth or republic, as a post state form of self-government." "Don't Trust The Man, Pigs Must Die!" Was scrawled everywhere in my neighborhood. If it were true or not, this whole "Democratic Socialism" was not a very smart thing to do back then. The riotous violence in August of the 1965-Watts Riots showed me, a 5-year-old child, how quickly the lives of so many people can change. One traffic stop, on one day and the world as we knew it would never be the same. Without change we would never succeed or grow. We had a revolution to free ourselves from British rule and it was extremely necessary, but this time there had to be a better way. When you are pushed and feel as though your back is against a wall, and on top of that you feel as though you have no place to go, then you fight! Watts was never the same after the riots as far as I was concerned, but could it get any worse? One of the largest and most notorious gangs in the United States was born in my back yard. "The Compton Crips." Again, challenges create competition, and competition sparks learning. I learned very early to watch my back and be extremely careful with the people I brought into my life. Making a friend back then created a bond that made our neighborhoods pretty strong. Looking at my life growing up in a challenging environment, being in it you don't see the challenges because they become commonplace. As these challenges continued to invade my life they made me stronger and more focused. By the way, the "Compton Crips" are still there!

LIFEWORK JOURNAL ENTRY

FOCUS was slowly creeping into my life like a stalker. It became a way of life for me and in turn, became a "Rite of Passage." That Rite of Passage became real and a very serious life experience for those close to me and myself. I lost a very close friend to gang violence James (Mickey)

Chamberlain. Mickey and I met in junior high school and we became the best of friends. Growing up without any brothers, I was a year and several months older than Mickey, so he was like my little brother. Making it to college first, Mickey was going to meet me at Cal-State Los Angeles and from there we were going to go to law school. This would be our ticket out of the hood. We talked about becoming lawyers, making lots of money and living the single life in LA. Life can change in a split second... Mickey was killed! Another victim of senseless gang violence and black on black crime. During the time between 1979 and 1985 gang violence in South Central L. A., Watts and Compton was at an all-time high. We found out later Mickey's murder was a case of mistaken identity. I will never forget Mickey and how having someone as close to me as a brother, changed my life. Many lives have been lost for no other reason than ignorance. After Mickey was murdered, I became even more focused with everything in my life. There were times when I got extremely angry thinking about losing someone so close to me. At times, and not by choice, I began to live my life in an angry state, and that would create depression, which at times would cloud my FOCUS. Mickey had a potential for greatness, so in his memory I refused to stray and I learned to control the anger that sometimes raged in me. Clint Eastwood, said "When you kill a man, you kill every opportunity he ever had!" As I got older I learned the system is sometimes not fair and not always as honest as we would like it to be. You don't have to completely conform to the system, but you need to understand how to work in the system. Learning how to work in the system known as "THE STREETS" is what you and those close to you did to survive where I grew up. The lessons' I lived through, not only taught me to be loyal to those I grew close to, but I also expected them to be loyal to me. This did become a serious Rite of Passage.

END LIFEWORK JOURNAL ENTRY

Every day I survived a challenge; FOCUS was developing in me. It also helped to keep me out of trouble. Staying out of trouble was extremely important because, my dad didn't play that. Not wanting to ever become a product of my environment, focusing on my schoolwork was extremely necessary. I also learned very quickly once you've truly learned something no one could take it away from you. Knowledge became my real power. Acquiring knowledge is one of the easiest lessons for survival. Whether it was book knowledge, or street knowledge you need to educate yourself. We live in a country, a nation, a universe, where information is free. The Internet is everywhere and around every corner information is at our fingertips. There is no excuse or reason, why you can't succeed at whatever it is you want to do with all of the resources we have at our disposal. I believe the more you learn, the more you should want to learn. Spending so much time in the library, learning became second nature for me. Success should never be measured by financial gain (MONEY). Money is a tool and if used properly will not only benefit you, but as a tool can be used to help others. This might sound a bit cliché, but "true success starts in your heart." Having a fire burning inside, igniting your passion and desire for something, is one of the true keys to your success. Everyone has his or her own personal feelings, or idea about success. The Passion, Drive and Desire, P.D.D. is what fuels your internal fire. It starts in your heart, but the end result is your dreams and hard work completed. Whatever the idea, whatever the feelings, you can't accomplish any of your objectives without understanding how to FOCUS. Knowledge can be infectious…

I completed and graduated, Manual Arts High School, class of 1978 with honors. Proud of my accomplishments in high school and because I worked so very hard, I was able to go to college. To my surprise, the college I attended, Cal State University L.A. was not a joke and this is where I received the first failing grade of my life. I'm not going to make any excuses, but Mickey's death ripped my soul apart during that time and I began losing my FOCUS. I began losing sight of this opportunity but needless to say I was devastated by the failing grade. I was able to buckle down and redirected my FOCUS. I got my grades and my study habits back up to par, taking full advantage of the knowledge I was being offered which created a great college experience. It gave me considerable understanding about life I could not have learned anywhere else. One of the greatest pieces of knowledge I acquired while I was in college was, "Limitations." I know, I know, what you're thinking "limitations?" Yes, limitations! This is my personal feeling because of the person I was then and the person I definitely am today. This institution of higher learning in many ways placed limitations on the creative thinking and positive imagery that is my life. I kept having internal struggles with my creative side and the structure of college. Sometimes certain places don't fit at certain times in your life. The great thing about having free will is just that… if you are strong in your convictions and are willing to sometimes stand alone, then you understand what I mean. I would never tell anyone not to attend college, especially if your parents are paying for it, and I would never say that going to a four-year university is not a good thing. It is a great place for those who have a passion in their hearts for learning that way, but some of us have to learn in a different way. Not because we want to, but I believe it's a part of our D.N.A. If you have an entrepreneur's heart, sometimes structure can stop or stifle your creative thinking. Living in the positive on a regular basis can cause you to become an individual! Standing alone can sometimes be a scary place, but it can be done. When I decided not to continue my studies in college my parents lost their minds! It's a good thing I was paying for it. Eventually they remembered who their son was and backed off. I have to say they've always trusted my judgment and allowed me to fall flat on my face, but they have always been there to pick up the pieces, if I needed them. At the end of my third year in college, I decided to leave. Mind you, I was doing well in college, but I think it got to a point that I was not able to maintain my FOCUS in college. Something kept gnawing at me in the back of my mind, in my D.N.A. At the time I made this decision, I was not sure why I did it but I just knew it was something I had to do. As time moved on, as it always does, I would learn the reason. I believe my leaving college had nothing to do with school and everything to do with my growth and development to becoming a writer. I didn't want to disappoint my parents, but there comes a time when we have to live our lives. I had the idea of being a writer during this time, but was afraid to express those feelings and mostly out of fear. I thought to myself, who was I to be a writer? My FOCUS was still in its early stages of development. One day I slowly began to realize I was not here to live my life for anyone else, but me! In many cases we spend more than half of our lives trying to please our parents. Believe me… I love my parents and there is nothing I would not do for them. As a parent I know our parents just want the best for us and the bottom line is, they just want us to be happy in whatever it is we want to do. I also learned that once you find FOCUS and understand "YOUR" reason for being it's never going away. It will haunt your subconscious and your conscious mind every day. You can choose to ignore it like I did for years, but just know it's going to keep rearing its persistent head until you finally take it by the horns and run with it! Trust me, I'm finally writing right? And I love it!

At almost 21 years of age, even as I went to college, I had to have a job to pay tuition. I've been working since the age of 14 and I used to think I was just a lucky person, but I soon realized the harder I worked, the luckier I got. Hard work is the key component in anything you do. Remember what I said about things happening in your life the way they were supposed to? Once I left college, I needed a good paying job to take care of my very young family. Oh, I forgot to mention, I got married at age 20 and that's truly another story.

I decided to do something I had thought about for a number of years. I applied for a job with the Los Angeles County Sheriff's Department. I had always been interested in law enforcement, but not so much as a lifelong career. I know it was something I had to do at the time. The Los Angeles County Sheriff's Department was the only law enforcement agency I considered, because they offered the largest variety of lateral movement of any department in a major city. They also had comparable pay to any of the other large police agencies, in Southern California. The Los Angeles County Sheriff's Department was also one of the best trained and one of the most respected law enforcement agencies in the free world. The testing process for the sheriff's department was a challenge, but it told me something about myself… in a word "Fortitude" (Strength of mind and endurance in a difficult or painful situation) comes to mind. If you didn't prepare, like 61 of my classmates decided not to do, you didn't make it! My Academy Class (210) started with 181 Deputy Sheriff Trainees and other Participating Law Enforcement Agencies. Only 120 of us graduated making the final cut and moving on into our law enforcement careers. "Eighteen weeks of living hell, just to work the county jail." You talk about FOCUS? Physical training: Running more than 5 miles per day, push-ups, pull-ups and sit-ups; everything was up! Courses of study: from the California Penal Code, to learning department policies and Radio Codes. Weapons Training: Learning to manipulate handguns and shotguns would become a part of my daily routine. Lectures on Los Angeles gangs… there go those "Crips" again. During an intense eighteen weeks of training, my

Drill Instructors and guest lecturers crammed so much information into my mind, my body and spirit if I didn't FOCUS I would have been out! I couldn't let that happen. Another opportunity presented itself and another challenge was met. Success again! I spent twenty plus years of my life in law enforcement on some level: I served twelve years with the Los Angeles County Sheriff's Department and seven years with the Inglewood Police Department on a full-time basis and three years as a reserve police officer, also for the City of Inglewood. My experience in Law Enforcement not only helped to shape the person I am today, it taught me again to FOCUS on so many levels. Taking advantage of every opportunity placed before or given to me…

LIFEWORK JOURNAL ENTRY

In several cases in my law enforcement career I had to learn to deal with certain situations. Even though I grew up in Watts and Compton there were many things I just had not seen or experienced. While in the sheriff's department I responded to a child abuse case. I remember thinking and a having million thoughts run through my mind. I expected when I arrived to see a child battered and bruised, and to my surprise, the little boy seemed and appeared almost normal. He didn't have a scratch on him and he appeared to be in good spirits. He was a little shy and withdrawn but his attitude was good. During my investigation the social worker explained to me that the little boy was suffering from, "FAILURE TO THRIVE SYNDROME." At the hands of his mother, her brother and her brother's wife, this little amazing boy was being treated as less than human. I had never heard of this syndrome. He was forced to eat, study and sleep in a very small space and was not given access to the rest of the apartment. The social worker also advised me he was the oldest of three. When I looked at his siblings I could clearly see he was much smaller than the two of them. Failure to thrive syndrome in this case happened through mental abuse. It caused the body's pituitary gland to shut down, stunting his growth, so he and his body could adapt to his environment (LIVING IN A CRAWL SPACE). At this point in my law enforcement career, this was one of the most devastating things I had ever seen. I'm using the example from my LIFEWORK JOURNAL as a lesson in courage. Even though this little boy was being abused in an unspeakable manner, he still managed to maintain an "A" average in school. Even today this still blows my mind! Without even thinking, this child was able to FOCUS during an extremely negative situation. He held onto his life the best way he could. He also found a way to see outside of the tragic world he was living in and found academic success. This situation also taught me even in the worse circumstances and we don't believe there's any way out, opportunities continue to be placed before you. After placing the adults under arrest, I was able to move the abused boy and his siblings to a very nice family in Malibu, California. I was extremely happy the siblings were able to stay together. I have to believe this young boy was able to live out the rest of his childhood in a safe and loving environment. I will never forget his fighting spirit as long as I live!

END LIFEWORK JOURNAL ENTRY

During my third year in law enforcement I was presented with an opportunity. I was working a day shift trade for one of my co-workers. I didn't really care for day shift, but he needed the day off so I made the trade. Again, things happen in your life the way they are supposed to. During my shift I made a traffic stop on a vehicle, traveling Westbound on Sunset Blvd at Doheny Ave. The vehicle was moving at a high rate of speed and after I made that traffic stop, my life began to change. The driver of the car was a respected artist, producer and businessman, in the music business (From Opportunity Comes Unlimited Success). I advised him to slow down and because it was so early in the morning and there was no traffic on the streets, I decided to "Warn and Advise" and send him on his way. He told me he appreciated my professionalism and he thought I would make a great addition to his security team. The artist was Lionel Richie. I thought he was blowing smoke, because he thought I was going to give him a ticket. He offered me a part time job, or as we call them "An off-duty job." He told me to contact his head of security and he would fill me in on the job and the duties, if I was interested. I didn't take him up on his offer that day. Approximately one week later a very good friend of mine (Linda Nesbit) contacted me about an off-duty opportunity to work a security detail for someone in the music industry. Guess Who? Lionel

Richie! Talk about things happening in your life the way they are supposed to. I thought to myself, an opportunity again was placed before me. I called his head of security and inquired about the job, and after several conversations; I decided to take a part-time position with his security team. This opportunity allowed me the chance to work in an extremely exclusive industry that I found very exciting. Being the hard worker that I am, it wasn't long before I developed a reputation in the industry for being extremely focused and directed in my duties. My reputation opened more doors, which led to more opportunities. I was able to pick and choose whom I wanted to work for. I even had clients making recommendations for my services. I developed a positive name in this business of personal security just as I had done in my law enforcement career. I can't help but think about my dad and seeing our name in a positive light. I began thinking to myself when I finished my law enforcement career I was going to start my own security company. I liked the freedom the job offered and I also liked being involved in personal security. Several years later, I made the decision to retire from law enforcement early and dive in head first into this world. There I was again being different. Having this side gig gave me the understanding I could do something on my own, "Have gun will travel." I was doing extremely well in my law enforcement career, as I had done in college. My name on both of the departments I worked for was synonymous with hard work and pride to duty. I had some truly great partners and I was a great partner. My law enforcement friends are just like the friends I made as a child, we trust each other with our lives and the bond in this instance doesn't get any stronger. I realized something about having a true friend… if you can't see yourself giving your life for that friend, or you know this person calling you their friend won't do the same, then stop calling people you meet and maybe hang out with from time to time your "friend." Call that person an acquaintance and there is nothing wrong with that, but I just want you to see the difference. This is just my personal opinion. I was able to work pretty much every detail I wanted, in the two law enforcement agencies I worked for. I truly enjoyed my job, but still I decided to make a change and walk away from my law enforcement career. I had nearly 20 years of training, growth and development and now I was moving out to explore the world of self-employment. Scary, but remember what I said earlier… law enforcement would not be a life-long career so I had to move on. Every moment is a blessing in so many ways! You're never quite sure if you made the right decision. Once you make a decision, right in your eyes and maybe wrong in someone else's, make it, stand by it and live with it! When I look back at many of the decisions I made, I realized I made them with an open heart and a full commitment so whatever I was going to do it was done! You have to visualize and believe whatever you decide to do you will be successful. All doubt must be eliminated from your spirit and you have to Focus Forward.

Having tasted the world of private security I found great pleasure and satisfaction with the living I've created. Not for the reasons you're thinking… not for the so-called glitz and glamour or the wild women and song. I truly enjoyed the freedom the job had to offer. The freedom started with one: being my own boss and not having a long list of people to answer to. Two: taking pride in the fact I created a job for myself and made myself a commodity. Three: I felt good about the responsibility being placed on my shoulders, good, bad or otherwise. As I said earlier we need "CHALLENGES" even if they are just to compete with ourselves. I was also proud of the fact that, when the opportunity presented itself, I was ready. During the time I was working in the private security sector, I took notes on every area of the business, from finance to manpower. I stayed on top of my mental and physical training. Continuing to learn about new technologies, weapons and anything else I thought would continue to make me a commodity. As I made contacts, I learned how to nurture those contacts and that nurturing helped me maintain those contacts years later. At present I have been involved in personal security for more than thirty years. During this portion of my career, I have done everything from: private bodyguard, consulting celebrities and major corporations on security systems and threat assessment, personal and corporate investigations. This career has been a Godsend and it has allowed me numerous opportunities. I have also been able to get involved in opportunities outside of security creating, inventing, and patenting fitness products just to name a couple, but my first love has always been writing. When I came to the realization I was put on this planet to write, I haven't looked back. As early as I can remember I've enjoyed being able to collect my thoughts by putting pen to paper. This is still the way I like to do it.

That's right, even in the age of the internet and computers, writing long hand is how I get it done.

Even though many of the situations I had to write about while in law enforcement were tragic, I took great pride in the fact that I was able to translate a victim's story into a viable report, to secure the conviction of a suspect. "Bad Boys, Bad Boys, what you gonna to do, what you gonna to do when they come for you?" I love that song. When you write you are able to create any person, feeling, situation, challenge or circumstance you wish. Writing has become for me "That passion for which I live and breathe." I can't get enough of it. This may all sounds a little mushy, but, I remember writing as a child and again not knowing what I was doing, I was laying the groundwork for not only my next career, but for my life's dream. I'm finally becoming, "Joe The Writer."

Over the years I have come to enjoy reading books about successful people. I've found they all pretty much say the same thing: Find something you enjoy doing or something you love and figure out a way to earn a living doing it and you'll never work another day the rest of your life. They never say "GET RICH" doing it or make billions of dollars doing it. The way I'm writing it may sound simple, but I believe, if something is in your spirit it's going to find its way to the surface, and when it does, it's best to know this particular opportunity is for you. It's kind of like someone having the acting bug deciding to take an acting class just for fun… that fun class could turn into a career doing something they love. Or let's say you love working out and you spend more hours in the gym than you do at home. Doing what you love, you decide to get certified as a trainer… you just created a job allowing you to make your own hours, do what you love and live your life the way you want to. Most people who take this journey, don't realize where they are going, because they're in the moment. They are living this life and because it's something new, they haven't learned the true meaning of the moment they are in. This passion that turns into a living can create a positive CHALLENGE that will assist you on your new journey. These positive challenges can also create a new LEARNING experience. There go those two words again: CHALLENGE and LEARNING, and if you're smart, you will continue to challenge yourself and learn from those challenges, for the rest of your life. FOCUS will also allow others to see how determined you are to make positive things happen. Remember, doing something you love to earn a living does not automatically equal millions of dollars, but I believe it does help to create an environment for you to be able to do so. When you love what you do and you have Passion, Drive and Desire, giving up will never be an option. Your spirit won't allow it! Believing in yourself is okay and you should never feel guilty about it. You need to believe your life is here for living and you're not just waiting to die. Everyday people go about living their lives, in what they believe is their success, only to discover they are living a lie. They are not following their true passion. Not that this is in any way a failure… it's just a minor delay to your success. My belief is, the more people that can live a life following their passion, the happier they'll be creating a better world for all of us to live in. Those are my thoughts and I'm sticking with them!

Most of us ask ourselves, who am I? or what can I do? We sit or stand in the mirror and pick ourselves apart from A to Z. Because of all the things we have going on in our lives, we don't allow our true "Essence", or our true "Spirit" to ever grow. Because we don't, we never get the answer to our question of being. Why are we here? As I grew older and started to understand my life, I realized my life had more of a purpose than I originally thought. Over the last several years, I finally understood living happy was okay. Living my life to the fullest 15 seconds at a time, enjoying every day the way I am supposed to. Waking up and being able to see with Clarity in Vision is something you must experience. I hope it happens while you're reading this book. The way I see life, I have to believe from the day I was born FOCUS was slowly developing into something tangible. As Clarity in Vision developed in me, I began to see a clearer path to the successes in my life. Every step made with caution, but there was an underlying feeling of confidence, if I took the first step the second step would be much easier. As long as I did my homework in every area of what I wanted to do, knowledge would always keep me moving Focus Forward. If success is what you make it, then let's make it happen. I'm not saying everything you touch is going to turn to gold, but I want you to get used to touching something! Don't be afraid to try. Being prepared in my life helped me to always be prepared in my job. Preparation always let employers know I was serious about my position in their company, and doing my job to the best of my ability would never come into question.

Obstacles and challenges are going to pop up all over your life, but if you prepare yourself, panic and stress will diminish. Look at your life this way… "If you're not doing anything you won't have any challenges to fuel the fire burning inside you." You have to be prepared to reprogram yourself. You have to be prepared to reprogram yourself. I said it twice to make sure you are paying attention. Since you're listening let's move on. As long as you live, two things are going to constantly change: Taxes and You! If you're smart, you'd better adapt. People do it every day. If everything were easy, the reward on the back end would be as flat as non-carbonated soda. We have to allow our mind, our bodies and our spirit to grow into a powerful light. You have to be open to the world around you. There is a light shining in all of us and that light has been dimmed, by the world you allow yourself to live in. The older we get the more set in our ways we become. It's not an easy thing to do, but we have to start learning some new tricks. I'm so happy as I got older, I was able to start seeing my FOCUS and understanding it. I'm happy the creative person I am, didn't die years ago. As a writer I am able to share this with everyone. I believe I have grown as a person because of it. I also wish the same for my family, friends and everyone I come in contact with. I'm not trying to preach to you or create some new religion. I just want you to know you can be happy. I also want you to know you have the tools to do this yourself. I have to believe this concept was given to me, so I could share it with you. You need to know you are as strong, and can be as focused, as you allow yourself to be.

Prepare to exit the Matrix. Why The Matrix? First: it's one of my favorite films. Second: if you've seen the Matrix Trilogy, the world as they knew it was not real. Neo, the lead character in this film, for all intents and purposes was there to save mankind. This was his life's mission and he had to learn to take advantage of every opportunity placed before him, but Neo also had to learn to believe in himself. As the trilogy developed Neo's character evolved, just as you must learn to do, because everything was constantly changing. Around every turn the agents have taken over the real world and pulled the wool over all our eyes. The Freedom Fighters fought the negative forces in their lives (THE MACHINES) so they could survive and just be happy. This is just a movie, but as movies go it's one of the greatest battles of good versus evil. I believe The Matrix, is one of the best, written screenplays of this time. I know this because I have acquired a copy of the first movie's script and each time I read it I discovered something new.

In this battle the "GOOD" is you. You're doing your best to make it through life with the least amount of resistance possible. Live and let live. Now the "EVIL," in your existence, is the negative effects of our society being placed on you from every corner of your day, from the time you were born. It seeps in through family, friends, co-workers, husbands, wives, children, and even that job you may be in right now. There is so much negative in our lives we've slowly allowed it to take over and then one day "YOU" realize "YOU" never had a chance to exist. Because it happens so naturally we can't see it, but we wind up feeling it… depression, anxiety, hopelessness, and an endless amount of negative circumstances. In many cases this is what we are left with and unfortunately this is the part of human nature we are supposed to live with. Or do we? Do we have to live in a negative world? Are we forever going to be stuck in this Matrix-like society? If you really dig deep, "Free Your Mind" and allow yourself to think freely, you might remember that single moment in time. The one moment you were at the crossroads and veered left when you should have gone right. This was the turning point that left you in the Matrix. It's not too late. It's never too late, but you have to want it! So, whatever, "IT" is you have to make up your mind to go after "IT" and don't look back. Once the characters in the story realized the Matrix, the world they thought was real was in fact a simulated computer program they learned the importance of reprogramming themselves and adapting to their new reality. They tried to find happiness in this new world, but they were not able to, so they decided to fight back! Standing up and fighting the machines trying to destroy them, is what they needed to do. That's all I want you to do… "FIGHT BACK!" The main thing they wanted was to continue to be human. Let "HUMAN" become your first thought every night before you go to bed and every morning you wake up. I don't believe it's on purpose, but most of us get so caught up in chasing numbers, we lose sight of the human factor. Whether it's the numbers in the money we want to make, or the number of people we can push through to attain our so-called goals or success, at times we lose sight of the "HUMAN" factor. The numbers just like "THE MACHINES" you'll only see the calculations and not the person. We have lost sight of everything human, so you have to learn to see yourself and those around you as a person again. You're going to have to look in the mirror and see the light inside yourself. It's always been there, but for many of us, mostly out of fear, you don't want to believe you could be happy and successful. The person next to you put in less work than you, but they have learned to believe they can do it. Like me they didn't know how to FOCUS, but they BELIEVE all things are possible. You may not want to believe you are here for a particular reason. You may not believe something good, that you could be in control of, could happen to you. You can allow the good to happen, or you can fight it tooth and nail like you've been doing forever and never succeed. Or you can allow yourself to know your destiny exists, because change is coming. When you learn to open you mind you will see a constant shift in your ability, to see a better you. A belief in your abilities will also manifest, when opportunities are placed before you. Your developing knowledge in the fact that things happen in your life the way they are supposed to and because they do, you can change your life for the better. You have to learn to stop, look and listen to the real world around you and allow every opportunity to take shape. I only have two more questions for you: Do you take the "BLUE PILL" close the book and continue living your life in the Matrix, not being able to ever see your life's true and full destiny? Or do you take the "RED PILL" and see how deep the rabbit hole goes? If you decide to keep reading, let's take a "look in the mirror" and see what it has to say, about you, your life and your destiny…

2

Look In The Mirror!!!

It is not the strongest of the species that survive, nor the most intelligent, but the one most responsive to change...

Charles Darwin

Well, well' well... look at you. I am so happy to see you decided to take the RED PILL. Now we're going to find out how deep the rabbit hole really goes. I know you just started chapter two and you're probably very curious and somewhat anxious to see what's next... but I need you to do me a favor; it might seem a little silly but humor me. I need you to find a mirror and stand in front of it. It's okay, I'll wait. You can take the book with you. Now that you're there, look at yourself for about four to five minutes. When you're finished with what you think is four to five minutes, pick up the book and continue with this chapter. Welcome back. Most of us have an extremely hard time standing and staring at ourselves in this piece of reflective glass. As young children, we look into and played in mirrors with an innocence, not judging ourselves, not worried about how we look, not ever thinking this piece of reflective glass that can't utter one word, would become our judge, jury and in some cases executioner. For some of us looking into a mirror every day is like a slow but sure death because of what we think we see. Montel Williams has been my main client for the last twenty years and I'm honored to say a trusted friend. He has a quote he uses when he's speaking that I have admired for years and it goes, "The tragedy of man, is what dies inside him every day that he or she lives." If you're superstitious, you should go ahead and break the mirror now and let what you think is fate, or nature take its course. I would hope that you keep reading. This tragedy happens through adolescence, the teenage years and then into full adulthood. All the baggage we collect and bring to the mirror with us every day, has us living our lives according to "what we believe we see and not what we once believed we could be." As young children we are fearless because we don't know we can't be. Then one day pieces of us start to die because someone; a parent, a family member, a friend, a neighbor, a classmate, a teacher, or even a stranger says one or two words that change the direction in your life, for what you "THOUGHT" would be forever.

This chapter is called "Look in the Mirror" for one reason and one reason only. I want you to look at yourself… IN THE MIRROR! Not just your face, but I want you to look into your eyes and don't turn away. I need you to be honest! When I asked you to look in the mirror for that four to five minutes, did you even look into your eyes? Most people can't or won't do that! I know it sounds crazy, but a large percentage of the population, don't really look at themselves in the mirror. When most of us do look at ourselves in the mirror, we don't look into our eyes. We look at the superficial parts of ourselves: our hair, our skin, a beard, our ears, etc., but we almost never look into our own eyes. Could it be we are afraid of what we may see? I sure was! The late, great Michael Jackson has a song called "MAN IN THE MIRROR." Several years ago, I don't remember exactly when, I began listening to it at least once a day, every day. Every morning while I'm in the gym it's the first song I play to begin my workout. I believe this song opens up my mind to the fact that "each day I'm allowed a new beginning to create a better me." My spirit, mind and body are realigned to work as a single unit so that I can achieve success. The beginning of the song goes… "I'm gonna make a change for once in my life. It's gonna feel real good, gonna make a difference, gonna make it right." These lyrics hit my heart one day and opened my eyes to seeing my world differently. My mind set every day is maintaining my FOCUS to make a difference in my life and the lives of the people I meet. More specifically I've learned to pay attention to the world around me because it's really easy to get lost in our own lives. The mirror can be a scary place for some of us because of our own internal reality. We could be afraid to exercise the demons so to speak, living inside us. Trust me we all have them. These demons have lived inside some of us for too many years now. They have forced us to live our lives like they are not our own. We have given our existence away, like it was for sale to the highest bidder… fear has become our ruler. We have become so good at manufacturing fear, it forces us to live in a constant state of confusion and self-doubt. One of the things that really scares me is, because we accept this way of life, we pass it on to our loved ones our husbands, wives, co-workers and even our children. You do have a choice and you can choose to live your life in the positive. CHANGE has to become your life's new vision, because change is coming. The quote at the beginning of this chapter, "It's not the strongest of the species that survive, nor the most intelligent, but the one most responsive to change." Your daily look in the mirror is there to help you Focus Forward, giving you a chance for a better outlook for your future. A true key to the mirror's importance is "YOU" being receptive and responsive to change. As you continue to read this book your opinion of yourself is going to change. At the moment, you may not be able to look into your own eyes because of the journey they may take you on. There is a quote that says, "The eyes are the window to the soul." The soul, which is comprised of your thoughts, feelings and most of all your will, could be a very scary room to sit in. The consciousness of our souls is what often times directs our feelings about ourselves. Free will, fortunately and unfortunately gives "YOU" the option of how you should, or want to feel. Most of us haven't learned to control those negative feelings. When I say control the negative feelings, I mean controlling what and how you react to things, but most importantly controlling, "WHAT COMES OUT OF YOUR MOUTH." What you say about yourself, whether out loud or in your head, is just as important as what you see in the mirror, or what you believe you see. Your thoughts play an extremely significant role in the direction your life takes. If you tend "NOT" to be happy with yourself, or your existence, looking at yourself in a mirror, could prove to be very difficult. Again, free will gives you the right to do, feel and say what you want. Think about it for a minute. Think about feeling and being positive. Think about seeing the positive side of your life. Think about saying positive things about yourself. So, wait a minute… you mean to tell me, I can pretty much do, say and think what I want, when I want? I can feel how I want when I want? You're probably asking yourself these questions and many more. The answer is, YES you can! You can be as POSITIVE or as negative, as you want to be about your life. It's your life not your boss, or your co-workers, or your spouse, or even your parents… it's yours! Your happiness is solely up to you. It's been said, "Ignorance is bliss," but because you know you have the ability to change your circumstance, you can't use it as an excuse anymore. There are "No More Excuses," for you to lean on, or hold responsible for what you are or not doing. As you begin to learn what you do POSITIVE, or negative affects the world around you, then and only then will you understand the mirror's importance. One day the mirror will not only show you your reflection; it will show you a better future.

I'm smiling as I write this paragraph, because I know how it felt when I realized I had the ability to change my life. Having a winning spirit is another step you will come to understand about yourself. As you begin learning to mirror yourself, your FOCUS will begin to paint a clearer picture of the opportunities placed before you. For me, clarity comes in many forms. I'll be speaking on four of them in this chapter. The point behind clarity is to help you see a clearer picture of your spirit. The spirit, which holds your confidence, or as I like to call it the "SOUL STEP," of each individual once strengthened, creates a bond with the Universe that I believe is unbreakable and unstoppable.

Clarity is a noun and is defined as:
1) The quality of being easily understood.
2) The quality of being expressed, remembered, and understood in a very exact way.
3) The quality of being easily seen or heard.

CLARITY IN THOUGHT: (CIT) THOUGHT, is s noun and its defined as: the action or process of: serious consideration, the power to imagine something that is. Clarity in Thought is developing a clear idea by having the power to imagine something that is before it is. Clarity in Thought will also give you the ability, to challenge yourself to believe beyond your circumstance, based on your thoughts. Your circumstances are just one thought away from changing!

"MAGIC MIRROR ON THE WALL;" Most of us have at some point

in our lives heard this phrase. If you haven't it's from the fairytale "Snow White." Now the queen in Snow White possessed a magic mirror, that when she asked "MAGIC MIRROR ON THE WALL, WHO'S THE FAIREST ONE OF ALL?" This mirror would respond by saying, The Queen was the fairest of them all. One day the mirror told her there was another fairer than she, "Snow White!" The Queen's thoughts of someone more beautiful than her drove her mad in the story. She "BELIEVED" what the mirror told her and my point is, most of us do the same thing every day by allowing the mirror we look into, to control our thoughts, thus controlling our lives. Let's figure out whom we are, by learning about why we are. Let's take control over what we see in the mirror by looking a little deeper into ourselves…

Everything we do begins with a thought. Everything you see before you began with a thought. The mirror you stand in front of every day began with a thought. Clarity in Thought is the sum total of a collection of thoughts, from infancy to adulthood that complete an idea. Positive or negative that thought is you. We watch them grow into a reality of tangibility each and every day. As you begin the daily process of looking in the mirror, your honest assessment of who you are will change through thought. The way you think about yourself are the thoughts you live with daily. If on a scale from one to ten, if one was less than the best and ten being the best of the best, where would you think to put yourself? I believe we have control over the thoughts of where we would put ourselves, but often times we don't exercise that right. So as a man or woman "THINKITH", so shall they be. It's time to change our thought process and look to see the positive side of where we should live.

Ask any person who believes he or she is great, or someone who has achieved great visible success, where would they place themselves on a one to ten scale and I'm sure they would put themselves at a nine or ten on that chart. Some of them may say nine because they don't feel their body of work is complete, but the "TENS" live that mindset every day. These people thought processes are always Focus Forward bridging the gap between doing and done and starting and finishing, but most of all they realize these positive thoughts are meant for them. When they look in the mirror they see completed task, a successful life, a successful future, a successful career, but most of all they believe the reality of success in every situation. They couldn't be negative even if they tried. They have also learned to speak their thoughts into existence or reality through daily, if not hourly affirmations. "Positive confessions breed believable professions." There is an old saying that I believe holds true today… "If you are what you eat," then you can also, "Be what you believe." The negative thoughts we see in the mirror are mostly based on fear. For years the "THOUGHT" of writing this book created a fear in my spirit I was not able to control. My main fear was "WHO WAS I TO WRITE A BOOK?" Or "WHO WAS GOING TO READ THIS BOOK IF I WROTE IT?" But by far my biggest fear was, "rejection!" Fear was buried in my spirit and it clouded every word of this book that was also in my spirit. Every word of every page in "Unlikely Destiny" was inside me waiting to get out, but fear kept the words at bay. I had to learn to separate the fear and keep my thoughts intact and fully functional. I learned to do this through daily affirmations by saying "I AM A WRITER, JOE PRYOR IS A WRITER, I WAS NOT GIVEN THE SPIRIT OF FEAR, ALL IT TAKES IS ONE YES." I would say this over and over with a conviction in my spirit so deep the affirmation began to out-grow the fear that surrounded it. One day something clicked in my eyes as I looked in the mirror, which struck a note in my soul, shaking my spirit (SOUL STEP) and I truly began to believe! One day I started writing because I truly began to have a "DEVELOPING BELIEF" in my ability to do something outside the box I lived my life in at the time.

Every thought produces some form of fear; big or small fear does exist. Because fear is one of our greatest enemies, we have a lot of experience running from it, or just not facing it. You have to learn everything about what creates the fear living inside you. One of the ways to do this is the daily exercise of looking into the mirror, creating perfect practice through affirmations that will help you face the fear living in your spirit. Not ignoring your fear will help you to exercise the demon so to speak, right out of you. Learning to cast fear out without losing the thought is what happens during the daily affirmations you choose to use. This will also break the mold that keeps you stuck in a "Matrix" like bondage of a negative world. You don't have to be superhuman strong to change, you just need to be willing or responsive to it. Open your eyes and look deep into your thoughts. See the reality that is you successful, confident, brilliant, accomplished and much, much more! Trust me it can be done.

Nothing we do in life happens overnight. These thoughts have had years to develop and manifest into the negative control centers that at times render us helpless. As fast as our children grow-up, it may seem like it, but it doesn't happen overnight. Weight lost or gained in similar fashion doesn't happen overnight. My point is you can't expect to change your thought processes overnight. Perfect practice through hard work is the only thing helping to create a better outlook and attitude about the life you want live. Learning to allow the positive images of each thought to develop is the work you must put in. Everyone who has a special skill or ability i.e.; math, science, sports, speaking, writing or even building an engine realized one day they were different for some reason. Whether they used the mirror to work through affirmations or they just talked themselves through it, they still had to do the work! If it were easy everyone would be able to do it without any effort.

Strength of mind develops through hard positive work and that, "DEVELOPING BELIEF" I spoke about earlier, helping you through change. A developing belief is, a constant forward motion of positive thoughts creating this change. Everything you think from this point forward will become your thoughts to do with as you please. YES, you have the right to put yourself any place you choose. Success and failure are just words but you give each life in your spirit according to how you react to them in thought. I began to believe in the reality of my thoughts, but most of all I began to believe in the words I spoke out loud daily. You have to hear the affirmations in order to believe they exist. Everything we see before us began with a thought. If in the spirit of the "TENS," they didn't believe their thoughts or allowed fear, doubt or a negative person to enter into the equation where would they be? Say everything until it gets deep into your spirit and then allow your spirit to help you create the reality that will be you. Keep looking into the mirror and the mirror will keep looking into a positive future, through thought allowing you to live with a better outlook on life, love, but most of all you.

CLARITY IN VISION: (CIV) VISION, is a noun and it is defined as: a thought, concept or object formed by the imagination, manifestation to the senses of something immaterial, the act or power of seeing, visible. To dream! Clarity in Vision is the act of making your thoughts visible, creating a reality through your imagination, dreams and thoughts to achieve your goals. A vision quest of sorts is said to provide a deep understanding of each individual's life purpose.

Most of us live our lives based on what we can see, touch, taste, feel or smell. Nearly everything we do is based on these five senses. If we lose one of these senses, our mind, body, brain function kicks into a higher gear especially if we lose our vision, in order to compensate for what the body believes it has lost. CIV is a portal or a door so to speak that will lead you to a new idea of vision. As you develop this new vision or a way of looking at your life, it all starts in the mirror, allowing us to see the vision necessary to move Focus Forward. Now we know a little bit about the power of the mirror through thought, let's look at how our vision affects what the mirror projects. Our clarity in vision allows our vision's quest to live.

Have you ever had a thought so visually stunning you thought you could reach out and touch it? Did this visual image also create a physical response or emotion, which seemed to open up new doors in your mind? Have you ever had a dream so vivid you woke up disappointed? I'm sure you have. We all have at some point in our lives. These visions are so clear we almost could not control our physical response to them. These thoughts and dreams create a vision so clear they can make us laugh, cry, smile, or even sweat! CIV allows us to bring our inner most thoughts through vision into a tangible reality, giving you the ability to walk through this open door and feel comfortable in this space. As I stated earlier in CIT, everything we do begins with a thought. That thought develops into a visual reality in our spirit, passing through our souls and finally the vision comes to rest in an almost physical view or metamorphosis in our mind. "WE SEE IT!" We've created them sometimes without even knowing it's a "Visible Reality," something; someday we will be able to touch. The mirror is key, in this clarity as you exercise your ideas to a new way of thinking, but most of all a new way of seeing who you want to be through your own vision. The power of suggestion is a great tool, so I suggest you start seeing your success when you look at you…

LIFEWORK JOURNAL ENTRY

One of the tools I always use in creating vision, allowing my mind see what I'm working for, is my cell phone. "Visual Tools" are great for feeding your spirit eliminating fear and negative ideas. I decided to delete all of the games from my phone, allowing me more room for pictures. I have taken pictures outside of Barnes & Nobles and several local bookstores in New York where I live and other cities I have visited, where my books will be sold. I've also gone inside the store and taken pictures of the section, "SELF IMPROVEMENT" where my books will be placed for purchase. I have also gone to the buildings of different publishers that will sign me, publish and promote my books. I also say out loud every day, "Once my books are published and released they are already New York Times best sellers!" You can use this technique in every aspect of your life. If you want a job at a particular company, take a picture of yourself outside the building or even inside the building's lobby, then collect your research, do your homework and Focus Forward to getting that job! Cell phones are great for more than just games and these are the only selfie's you should be taking. I believe, "If you take care of business, business will take care of you."

END LIFEWORK JOURNAL ENTRY

If you were born blind or if you were, as Montel would say, "Differently Abled," your vision is still attainable. Look at Helen Keller or Stevie Wonder; even though they see the world differently than we do, their lives are more complete than many of ours. Montel was diagnosed with Multiple Sclerosis in 1999 and even with that diagnosis his vision for his life has not changed. He alone owns the definition of who he is, period! CIV allows each of us to have our own vision for who and what we want to be. Take a look in the mirror with your corrected 20/20 vision and make a decision to start seeing whom you can be. Ray Charles lost his vision at a very early age but never lost sight of what he could be. He didn't roll up in a ball in the corner and give up. Ray put in the work and learned what he needed and became one of the music industry's biggest Icons. My point is you don't need to physically see to have a vision or a thought. You do need to bring your thoughts and the idea of your vision, into action through positive daily affirmations, allowing your visions to come to fruition. I love and listen to music every day and because of music videos and live concerts it's very easy to put a vision behind the songs you like. Just like those music videos, I sometimes give my thoughts life; by playing them in my mind as a movie or a play in order make them real. As I stand in the mirror looking into my eyes, I will often close them once I have the visual, increasing the clarity through my spirit. Our minds are incredible on so many levels, but unfortunately, we barely tap the surface, of its full ability or potential. You have to allow your mind to work, by giving it work to do when you use vision as a tool for change.

Looking into "YOU" is extremely necessary in the mirror. Learning to forgive what you see in the mirror has to become a priority, but learning to find strength in that forgiveness is the next step on this journey. Forgiveness and strength are key factors in my "TREE OF LIFE." The faster you heal from what you think is wrong will enable you to create CIV. Nelson Mandela created a vision of forgiveness in his spirit, by hating oppression so much it allowed his vision to be clearer, or CIV to forgive his oppressors. CIV allows you to see your reflection, which is the physical vision, you see at first glance, but as you continue to purge your SOUL STEP, the windows will slowly open to your new and improved reality, creating your vision. Every day the vision develops clarity, of unmistakable substance. This substance given to you is understanding opportunities through thought, given to you by design are meant for you, not just as a thought, but also for your vision's reality. CIV is not some freak accident. It's the Universe attempting to give you something meant specifically for you. The biggest CIV stopper for most of us is the word NO! During your life you may hear the word NO more than a million times, and more than half of that million times it forms in our own mind. It's a defense mechanism, programmed into most of us at birth that I believe was our introduction to the Matrix. We believe it was put in place to protect us and in some areas of our lives its does the job it was meant to. In other situations, it has the ability to stop you from living a much fuller life, the life you were meant to live; the life you born to live!

When I look in the mirror I always tell myself, "YES, I CAN," whatever it is, it can be done. The word "NO" to me will always be "NEXT OPTION," which makes me even more determined to succeed. My belief is the word NO has opened more doors than most of us think. NO creates determination, fortitude, courage, and strength of mind and in many cases a more focused attitude to pursue your dreams. Next Option! Remember each dream becomes the vision sparking the thought that we mold and shape into a physical reality. CIV allows me to maintain a positive attitude about my life, because it keeps me in-line with what I believe and it does not allow me to live the circumstances that sometimes surround me. It also gives me perspective of the people I meet and that helps me to keep everyone in their own lane in life. NO in many cases is escorted through our spirit with fear. No, I can't do anything! No, I'm not qualified for that job! No, she's out of my league! These are just some of the phrases purging our minds in an attempt to protect us from pain or discomfort. Open your eyes to the vision that you are here to achieve greatness on many levels and reaching for that greatness may be uncomfortable, but should not be out of character, or out of your belief system. See yourself in a better life. See yourself doing everything you've always dreamed of, but most all keep your heart humble, your spirit free, your mind strong and continue to believe in your purpose. All it takes is one "yes" to fulfill a dream. The thoughts and visions we are given are good for us, and we have to believe they are meant for us. Sometimes we distort them when we allow fear to disrupt the thought, eliminating our ability to develop CIV. Remember what I said about fear and eliminating it from thought? If you don't work at eliminating the fear you won't be able to continue your journey. Allowing what you see to move Focus Forward and staying positive takes a lot of work, but anything worth truly having is worth the effort and the work you put in. Keep your vision's quest within reach by learning to see it, in the mirror and then in your spirit. Once you have any vision in your spirit it's not going to just fade away. It has been installed like a downloaded file to be accessed whenever you are ready. Minus the fear.

CLARITY IN MEMORY (CIM) MEMORY, is a noun and is defined as; the mental faculty of retaining and recalling past experience, something remembered from the past, a recollection. CIM is simply learning to use the memories you've collected, to your advantage in order to shape a better future for yourself. Having my sci-fi mind always at work, I look at memories as files or downloaded information into our spirit and stored there until they are needed.

As I look back at the thoughts and visions we collect as memories, I believe, they have created the path we live our lives on today. I believe these memories good or bad drive our lives in the direction they're in today. The successes and failures we experience are also logged into our memory banks to help us but in some cases hinder our Focus Forward progress. They hinder us because they don't allow us to see new opportunities that have been placed before us, because of our sometimes-clouded negative past. Our memories are more important than we think. Every bit of information, everything we've experienced from the time we are born, from the first voice we hear, or the first time we hear our own voice has been stored away in our spirit. Most of us think memories are stored in our mind, but they run a lot deeper than that. They are so deep in some cases they can evoke a physical response from our bodies that at times, can paralyze us with fear. "We are in many cases the sum total of what we remember and we often become what our memories give us." CIM can be an extremely effective tool once you learn to tap into it. You use your memory every day without any real thought; how you get home, or to school, recognizing family, friends or co-workers, remembering notes that you study for a test, I think you understand what I mean? As you look in the mirror this is the only time I want you to look directly at your face. Look at every line, freckle, bump, hair, or what you think maybe an imperfection. Remember the first time you looked at your own face. Look at it from the base of your chin to the top of your forehead. This is you… a perfect picture and the clearest image of you, that you have remembered, that you now remember, that you will remember. Your CIM needs to be based on accepting change. Change that will allow you to analyze your memories by dissecting them with clarity to understand, why you did or made many of the decisions you have to create these memories. Now let's look into those eyes and allow your memory to go to work. Take the most recent situation that has become a memory for you. You went left, but deep down in your spirit you know you should have gone right. You make a correction in your spirit so you don't make that same mistake again. This is a major part of that defense mechanism we are born with, but that memory has been logged away waiting for you to do it again. Most of us won't keep touching a burning flame because we know we'll get burned, but we are human. In order to create a new world for ourselves we have to break the negative memory mold so to speak and start learning to live the life we are designing for ourselves. Breaking the mold that protects us is going to take a lot of hard work and it all starts with understanding the word "NO" is not the final word!

Most of the NO'S attached to our memory are connected to negative situations we've already experienced. That defense mechanism I spoke about earlier, set in place by our mind, body, and brain function to protect us from outside forces and other times it protects us from ourselves, so we don't continue to make the same mistakes. One of the things I've learned is if it's already happened you can use everything in your memory as a blueprint to make changes in your life. A little tweak here and there is what you need to be open to. This reprogramming will help what your memory stored as a mistake and allow you to see outside the box that we sometimes get lost in. I understand our mind, body and spirit trying to protect us, but in order to effectively change or reprogram a memory you must look at and understand, what created the negative side of your memories. Earlier I wrote about how we react to the situations in our lives is what will dictate what happens, this also applies to our memories. Memory can only be given life if we bring them to the surface. We need them, most of us want them as long as it's not the bad ones, but memories good and bad are there for a reason.

Getting back to NEXT OPTION and how it helps you with memory control. I said earlier using my Sci-Fi mind, memories are downloaded files and if we had any unwanted files in any of our electronic devices, we press the DELETE button to get rid of them. They leave the desktop that is your mind, but bits and pieces known as "COOKIES" are much harder to get rid of. These are the bits and pieces of an incident left in your spirit. Our memory has to be looked at in the same way. A mistake set in your memory may not be completely deleted, but in time you will learn to work through and deal with certain negative situations as your FOCUS increases. Have you ever watched a sporting event: Boxing, MMA Fights, Basketball, Football, Baseball, Track & Field or Swimming and some of the best athletes competing in these events make a mistake early in competition, regroup and in their final push they're able to "DELETE" the mistake to come back and win? The point is because you can't completely erase the memory, how you respond to it makes all the difference in succeeding.

Michael Jordan, Steffi Graf, Venus and Serena Williams, LeBron James, Peyton and Eli Manning, have all faced adversity at the point of near failure then come back to win it all. These athletes and many others do the same thing every day by taking, the next option and creating a way to over-come a circumstance or adversity. In a game or in real life situations you need to always look for the next option. In order to delete a mistake, you've made you have to keep the memory present and remember "IT'S NOT THE END OF THE WORLD." We all make them and we will continue to make them but own it, file it away and move on. Learn to live beyond any mistake by not letting that mistake control your life forever. If you keep the memory present it allows you the opportunity to deal with it on a conscious level. Not allowing your subconscious to run or rule your life keeps everything you've learned available, always sharp and on point! Every memory we have is relevant to each of us. I would never discount or make light of anyone's memory especially the ones that have ruined lives or changed the course of someone's future, but my mindset in every situation is to "NEVER STOP TRYING!" Every day we look in the mirror searching for the mystery behind our eyes, looking at everything we can remember retracing some of the steps that haunt our memory and keep us in mental debt. Mental debt with checks that we can never cash. CIM can be an effective tool as you look in the mirror. When you get a clear understanding that memories can aid in changing the course of your life, from negative to positive you will not fear the word "NO" in the real sense. From this day Focus Forward "NO" will always equal NEXT OPTION, and that mindset will always give you the opportunity to win.

CLARITY IN OTHERS: (CIO) OTHERS, is a noun and is defined as: one that remains of two or more. A thing opposite to or excluded by something else. Clarity in Others is the ability to see and understand the people in your life, the people you'll meet and why you've met them. It will also give you the strength to make the decision of whom you need to keep in your life and whom you need to let move on. Clarity in Others is all about one of the mirrors biggest reflective enemies, "PERCEPTION." How do you see yourself and how do others see you? As I look in the mirror what do I see? When I first began this exercise of looking at myself in the mirror this is what I would always asked myself. There were days when I would stare at my reflection for over an hour, trying to figure this out. Before learning to control the bulk of my thoughts, vision, and what I allowed to be brought forth from my memory, or the downloaded files, everything was pretty much negative based. At first glance the perception came from a file storage box of everything said directly to me, or what I heard second, third or even forth hand, from: your ears are big, your nose is huge, you're too black and too skinny and to top it off, growing up in Watts and Compton Ca. most of my childhood, living way below middle class was also devastating and extremely tough to deal with. These are the thoughts, visions and memories that came to my mirrored surface daily. Now I go back to "PERCEPTION." If this is what I believed I saw or was, this is what I believed others saw and believed me to be. That sucks right? Living your life trying to figure out how others perceive you to be, is what most of us do and for what? CIO has more to do with you than it does with them. I know what you're thinking? If it has more to do with me then why didn't I call it Clarity in You? (CIY) Mainly because ninety percent of us, give or take a percentage point care what "OTHERS" think about us, from: how and where we grew up, what we are wearing, where we live, what we do for a living, who we are dating, who we marry and most of all who we pray to… I could go on for the rest of this chapter but I think you get it. The only ones who don't care about any of this are the "TENS", on that one to ten scale, because they are born programmed to win and don't waste time worrying about it. That's why a majority of them are successful! For the rest of us it requires a little bit more work to leave the house. One of the first things I want you to do is stop worrying about how others perceive you. Most people are going to see and believe what they want to anyway, so you may never win that argument in their minds.

Perception is a noun and is defined as: the organization, identification and interpretation of sensory information in order to represent and understand the environment.

If we look at the perception of our environment, our environment is every place our body physically takes us or inhabits and a major part of our environment will always be the people we invite into it. Anyone other than the family we are born into and raised with, is an invited guest and they become a part of our physical perception. When you think of the feuding families, The Hatfield's and The McCoy's the physical perception is two families that truly hate each other. This feud went on for so many years that if there was a change and these families decided to let their children play together no one would believe it, even if they saw it. Who you decide to spend time with or allow into your world has always been your decision. There is a saying that, "With age comes wisdom" and that wisdom gives you the right to remove negative people from your environment or your physical perception. I love this wisdom thing right now. There is another saying I just want you to think about, "WE ARE OFTEN TIMES JUDGED BY THE COMPANY WE KEEP." Think really hard about this one.

LIFEWORK JOURNAL ENTRY

As children we have no idea the amount of wisdom and intuition our parents have earned. Looking back, every person my parents told me to stay away from because they were nothing but trouble, pretty much turned out to be correct. Several times when I was running with the wrong crowd, my mother or father would call for me to do something or they'd send my sister to come and get me. I would find out later that one or two of my friends got into some sort of trouble. Sometimes something major happened and people were arrested and other times it was minor trouble, but trouble is trouble. This happened time and time again. Accident, coincidence or was it all by design. My belief is it was all by design. I also have to believe it led to me writing Unlikely Destiny.

END LIFEWORK JOURNAL ENTRY

I spoke in chapter one about developing many of the friendships I had as a child and as an adult. I've been blessed by and I hope a blessing to everyone in my environment and to those I meet in the future. CIO as it relates to the mirror is truly a reflection of you. We have to at some point take responsibility for the people we invite, share, and cultivate relationships with on every level. Whether personal or business it is our responsibility to bob and weave through the muck and mire of fact or fiction. I can tell you for the next ninety years that "I LOVE YOU" but, if my actions don't show or dictate "LOVE," wisdom should give you the courage to stay or go. The relationships we develop, create the friendships that become our environment. These friendships often create unique scars on our hearts, minds, and spirits. Good or bad, over the years we sometimes develop and become, what we see in the mirror. Don't allow a distorted view of who you should be, be taken away by an outside influence. Over time I've come to learn a few things about myself; I know everyone I meet has been placed on my road or in my path for a specific reason. Some of the people we meet we will know right away, why they are in our lives. They will be like-minded and on the same page with our thoughts and visions, helping us to create some incredible memories. Walking this path as I meet each passerby, I don't know why I've met him or her, but I've made it a point to treat everyone no matter where society has placed him or her as equal on every level. This is the way I know I should be treated! Others you meet, you will develop associations with, not friendships right away and that's ok because, one, two, five or ten years from now your meeting could come full circle. You guys will be able to help one another accomplish goals you have both set because your initial meeting was perfectly planned for your future. We meet everyone for a reason. Each person has a purpose and a point for being in our lives. The sooner you realize this, the sooner you can Focus Forward to completing your goals.

CIO allows you to develop strength in character, to look inside yourself and create a world better suited to live and thrive in. We have a habit of keeping every bit of ourselves in a neat little box shoved in a corner. We are in many cases afraid to think let alone venture outside this box and every creative thought, vision or memory stays boxed up forever, never allowed to become a reality. I can't allow myself to believe we live everyday just to get up, go to work or school, and go back home at some point, just to do it all over again the next day. You have to believe that your point and purpose are larger than you've allowed yourself to think at this point. Growing up can be rough and at times extremely unpleasant, but as long as you are alive, you can make a change. Every day is going to be a fight, but fear not you are a fighter! You fight every day to make your mark in this world and a set back here and there creates the "NEXT OPTION." CIO can be your roadmap to better understand, who, what, how, where and why you are, but most of all why you've made some of the decisions that could have your life in a tailspin.

LIFEWORK JOURNAL ENTRY

I was told by a very wise man one day, that the only bad thing about relationships is, "You have to get to know people in order to get to know people." I kept quiet on the outside but trust me, I was a little confused. The deer caught in headlights look must have passed through my spirit and onto my face, because the person who said this to me began to laugh. So, I said "Okay, I give up what does it mean?" I was about nineteen years old when this was said to me and I will never forget what that phrase means. If you don't remember anything else in this chapter, remember this… "You have to get to know people, in order to get to know people." This person was in his mid-thirties and at nineteen the mid-thirties seemed old, so I hoped he knew what he was talking about. He finally said to me "No matter the person: family, friend, boyfriend, girlfriend, husband or wife, even your parents, or children, getting to know someone is a process and it takes time. Sometimes years will pass and you still don't know these people?" Okay, so I think I'm getting it. Getting to know people is a process of growth. We grow at different levels and the dynamic of every relationship changes from year to year, so relationships just take time! Every day in the process of getting to know this individual, you are also learning more about yourself. A major part of the learning curve is keeping an open mind to learn. It also let me know that as we grow, we change. Our belief, our tolerances and lack thereof may change. As we become adults our relationships with our parents is going to change. As our children become adults our relationships with them is going to change and because of this our ability to understand ourselves and others will have to change.

END LIFEWORK JOURNAL ENTRY

CIO kicked me in the head like a mule! I really began to feel like Neo from the Matrix, seeing the "Whole World" for the very first time. I made it a point to keep my opinion of others at a one, leaving myself room to grow into relationships. I realized that you control the clarity at which you see people and as you get to know them you can determine where they fit into your life, or where you fit into theirs, positive or negative. As I look back at my life in New York, coming from Los Angeles, I had to make many adjustments, from living in an apartment in the middle of the city, to riding the subway on a daily basis. I had to learn the ways and customs of so many people on a personal and professional level very quickly, if I were going to survive. The first few months living here I was not happy because people didn't seem to like me. People walked by and didn't speak to me, or each other. At a point I stopped taking it personal. I knew it had nothing to do with me, but everything to do with each person's personal environment. Everyone was eyes front and off on their next mission. The way I perceived my environment didn't allow me to see with any real clarity. I decided to change my approach as I entered each day, by keeping my attitude positive and this allowed me to remain Focus Forward. I slowly changed the attitudes of almost everyone I came into contact with. My smile was able to receive smiles back. My positive attitude also received a positive response. I was able to control my immediate environment and I also realized we have more power over how we react to situations. WE HAVE THE POWER! You wouldn't have been afraid to stand-alone or really care what people say about you. Just look at the TENS. What people say about you and what you know is true, are two completely different things. There are times when you will be forced to stand-alone and because of the person you have become, standing alone should not cause you to lose your mind. When I first moved to New York I felt as though I had to stand-alone and for the most part I did. I put myself on an island and I also realized I had to find a way off that island... and I did. Take a deep breath, in and out, and as you remember to reflect in the mirror looking into your spirit, be secure in the fact that you are never alone. As long as you are able to summon the fire burning inside you, you will never fail. You have to start seeing your life through open eyes.

If you see yourself in "OTHERS" that you have chosen to associate with, work with, or befriend, this will give you a pretty good idea what direction you're moving in, or where you'll wind up!!! I asked the question "What do I see when I look in the mirror?" My mirror reflects me; positive, directed, motivated, a strong individual, on track for greatness and always Focus Forward. Remember what I said earlier in this chapter about the mirror? "One day the mirror will not only show you your reflection, it will show you a better future." We are amazing creatures, but we just have to learn to accept that we can be! Everything you've been through has brought you to this point of reflection, (No pun intended) and none of it has been a waste of time. You have to learn to live your life with no regrets, because you can't change anything about your past, but if you're serious about your future you can learn to live it better! I could go on and that is what I want you to do… go on! As you look in the mirror learn to believe in the positive side of what you see, you'll begin to see with clarity, creating a tangible reality. Look in the mirror, close your eyes. Now open your eyes. When you open them, scan your face from top to bottom. Looking at your face, look back into your eyes and find the place that brings you peace. That peace will lead you to your Soul Step and your true spirit! Since I have you looking in the mirror a little more comfortably, with a little bit more confidence, my next question to you is "Why are you here?"

3

Why Are You Here?

If I had one wish for my children, it would be that each of them would reach for goals that have meaning for them as individuals.

Lillian Carter

"Why are you here?" That's such a loaded question… "why are you here?" A major part of why I believe you are here, is to live your life to the fullest and create amazing memories. You may be here to discover a cure for cancer or the common cold. You could be here to raise a child, who could be the next President of the United States. That's not really the question I'm asking you; it's the question you should be asking yourself. In my introduction I told you about the 45 seconds that changed my life. I realized that day my idea of my life would never be the same. I also told you I would live my life 15 seconds at a time, enjoying every moment of every day with the feeling it could be my last. We have no idea what the next few moments may bring. I really want you to think about your existence and your reason for being. The life force, which makes you who you are, what's the point of it? I clearly and completely know why I'm here and what I'm supposed to be doing. I'll ask you again, what you should be asking yourself… Why are you here?

Being the person that I am, I've asked myself that question numerous times; as a child, a teenager, a young adult and as a man. As a teenager when I asked myself that question, I really didn't think much about it.

As a young man, I really asked the question because of where I grew up. I found myself sometimes feeling hopeless. The hopelessness I sometimes felt was because of the circumstances surrounding my life at the time, but I never ever thought to give up! Growing up in Watts and Compton, California was sometimes a challenge. Thank God for me I found FOCUS, but nevertheless I continued to ask myself, why am I here?

LIFEWORK JOURNAL ENTRY

I remember telling my parents when I was about twelve years old; I didn't think I'd live to be 30 years old. On the morning of my 30th birthday, when I spoke with my parents, my dad reminded me about what I had said about not living to see 30 years old. All I could do was smile and I thought back to when I made that statement. By the time I was 30 years old I was living a good life and enjoying every aspect of it. I had a good job; my family was in good health and to this day I think I have the best friends in the world. L.G. Life's Good! but deep in my spirit I still asked myself, why are you here? I wondered about it until I was thirty-three years old. One day, clarity in thought the answer hit me like a ton of bricks. I am a "LISTENER." That may not seem like much to you but when you need someone to talk to and you really want someone to listen, you will understand. I'm the next best thing to a therapist without the bill. I listen to the problems of other people not by choice, but as a part of my destiny.

END LIFEWORK JOURNAL ENTRY

As I look back over my career and my life, every job I've held I had to interact with the public on some level. Whether working in retail or grocery, which was one of my very first jobs, or law enforcement and my current profession, private security, I have been a listener. Whether it was a customer, victim, suspect or the client, I've always handled and discussed situations that people sometimes didn't want to talk about, but they still chose to speak with me about them. As a cop I had to take and handle reports that sometimes turned my stomach and at times made me extremely angry. As I listened to the details of the crimes, of some of the suspects I interviewed, in my mind I'd beg for just 10 minutes alone with them, but in disgust, I listened. Did I learn to listen? Or was I born to listen? I believe some people, if not all of us are pre-destined to do most of what we do. If you are born with certain abilities even though they haven't developed to their fullest, they are there. Because of free will we don't have to do anything we don't want to. That's why some people don't develop their talents or abilities. If you are born with an ability giving you a ninety-five percent edge over everyone else, this ability could be why you are here. I believe you still have to put in the work to develop the ninety-five percent ability you have been given. So, when you think about it, with a five percent push you could move to the next level with minimal effort. Five percent effort could be your stepping-stone to personal, and professional success. Most of us don't recognize what we do could be a precursor from our D.N.A. It could be who we are, but some of us go on about our lives never knowing who, or even trying to find out why we are here? Well I think it's about time you ask yourself again… Why are you here?

Well did you ask? Don't worry it's ok you don't bite. Ask yourself again. Why are you here? Am I getting on your nerves yet? Am I driving you crazy? Have you reached the breaking point? The reason I keep pushing you on this question is I really want you to take the time and think about it. If you FOCUS hard enough maybe clarity in memory can be your guide. Think about your life, no matter how young or old you are, sometimes your memories can be the key to finding out why you are here. Understanding the negative side of your life can also be a useful tool and can shed a lot of light on why you haven't been able to solve this mystery. It can also allow you to understand why you are where you are right now.

We all have to earn a living, but you have to know in your heart and deep in your spirit there is something you are meant to do, more so than what you are doing right now. Keeping in mind because you have free will, you have chosen in many cases, to ignore the direction you should sometimes go in. This doesn't mean you are not or will not be successful. This only means the clarity you see with, will be a little cloudy without FOCUS and in that cloudy state, you will not be able to move Focus Forward at a proper pace. The more delayed you are in your success; your ability to help others is postponed. Your destiny is not only about you it's about not missing your ability and opportunity to help someone else. Discovering your destiny is about understanding your true potential, as to why you are here. I've learned as a listener, I couldn't control what people told me. You can to a degree decide what you want to hear or listen too. Since I was the one doing the listening, at times I felt compelled to give advice. I would often think to myself "Me giving advice… Are these people crazy?" As young as I can remember, as far back as grade school, other kids would share their problems with me. Clarity in Memory… I know you're thinking "Grade school?" Yes, grade school and it may seem a little hard to believe but it's true. Think about your life as far back as you can and if you do, I promise you, you'll start to see things about yourself, certain patterns you either forgot or didn't realize. There's something you do without thinking that could possibly be why you are here. When you think about this don't complicate it because, it could be something as simple as having a great rapport with children. Or you might be a stockbroker, with a flair for "Interior Design" or maybe you want to start a restaurant? Whatever the ability, you need to take note, even though you are given these abilities, they never develop overnight. Their development takes time and can only really start developing when you truly recognize and accept you have them. As I grew older, I experienced things that made me take step back, and shake my head. I had family; friends, suspects, strangers even clients tell me some extremely personal and incredible things. Some I wanted to hear because many of these people were close to me and I was genuinely concerned and others not so much, but nevertheless I listened. I had gotten to a point in my mid to late twenties where I stopped listening and I also refused to give advice. Listening began making me into angry person! The anger I was living began to overwhelm me. Yes, you can live in an angry state. Some of the people you know, family or even those you work with on a daily basis, live their lives in an angry state. Anger! Anger! Anger! I was becoming one of these people. Back then, like today, I was one of the most positive people walking this earth and I was losing it. People who find themselves always angry believe they are supposed to live this way. Remember what I said about the circumstances that sometimes surround or plague our lives? We get so used to them and in some cases, we believe there is nowhere for us to turn. I was falling into such a deep hole and I didn't know how to pull myself out, but I just didn't want to listen anymore!

As I write this I find it kind of funny, because the more I tried to resist listening, the more I was approached. I felt as though I had a sign on my forehead that said, "tell me your inner most personal secrets" and there was nothing I could do to stop them. One day I literally said out loud, "Why Me?" People kept confiding in me, sharing relationship secrets they wouldn't even talk to their significant other about. I got so angry about the situation, I found myself getting depressed. I want you to think about this for a minute…when you get depressed about other people's problems you begin losing your FOCUS, and I did. The confidence I had developed and lived my life by was gone. I began to feel the hopelessness I sometimes I felt as a child, growing up in Compton.

LIFEWORK JOURNAL ENTRY

One night as I tried to sleep, the tossing and turning woke me up. I got out of bed and went into my bathroom. I left the lights off as I stood in front of the mirror being lit only by a night-light. Looking into my own eyes trying to figure out, what was wrong with me? With the night-light on I was able to see the outline of my face and I could clearly see inside my eyes like it was daylight. I stood in front of that mirror for over an hour. Now as you know, I look in the mirror every day, as a part of my routine to maintain my FOCUS, but this was something different. Whatever I was looking for, I decided I was not going to leave that mirror until I found it. This was the first time I looked into the mirror and I began to see my "Soul Step" grow. I began to get this sense of calm and, the calm that came over me presented itself on my face. This was the same calm I felt when I flat lined for forty-five seconds. The intensity, which normally crunched my forehead, began to slowly disappear. As I think back during this time, I can make light of it now, but at the time it wasn't funny. I felt this chill run through my body from the top of my head to the souls of my feet. The anger that found a place to dwell inside my spirit began to shrink. The depression I was experiencing also felt as though it was beginning to fade. Looking back, I realized the depression was something I had to go through. This is one of the situations I spoke about earlier and I will continue say, "Things happen in your life the way they are supposed to." During this point in my life the things I went through, was a race I had to run by myself. I had to experience them, to be able to grow and fully understand the true essence of, "THE MIRROR."

END LIFEWORK JOURNAL ENTRY

As you live and move forward in life, you will discover that there are some things "YOU" have to go through period! The good thing about going through crap is getting through to the other side of it. Enlightenment is one of my favorite words because once I discovered its existence I realized I was moving forward and not stuck in the same place repeating the same mistakes. I am not empowered because no one had to give me power or authority over my life but, I am Enlightened because during my life process, I gained understanding about myself and I have been able add a positive spirit, to my existence. Albert Einstein said: "We can't solve problems, by using the same kind of thinking we used, when we created them." Once I left the mirror and sat down at the dining room table, I had an epiphany! I learned something very important about myself that morning… "When there is something in your spirit you must do, the longer you stall, wait, avoid, or just plain ignore doing it, it's not going to go away." Fighting what could be your destiny will create more stress in your life. I began to grow inside and I realized, it is not wasted time because every minute lived is just that, a minute lived, creating growth. If something is in your spirit it's becoming, if it's not already, a part of your DNA, and trying to change your chromosomes is just not going to happen. What you can do is change your mindset to the positive. I discovered that LISTENING is what I am here to do. As much as I didn't want to listen, I have learned to process other people's feeling as though they were mine, but I have also learned to keep them separate from my own. I have no idea how I do it, but I do. I can honestly say because I have accepted my ability, my life has never been better. It's almost like being a super hero. There's Batman, Superman, and Joe the Listener. "To whom much is given, much is required." When you struggle with something internally, deep in your spirit you limit your ability to move forward in every area of your life and the positive signals are not allowed to go through and your FOCUS becomes clouded. Your spirit is a powerful tool and when you try and muffle or keep it under wraps, it's going to find a way out.

My Anger and Depression have developed into what I would like to call Enlightenment. (I will elaborate more on Anger Depression, and Enlightenment in Chapter 7) I learned something very clear that day… talents come in many forms and even though you are given something you may not recognize as a talent in the beginning, if it keeps coming back to you then it's probably something you need to give a little more attention to. It's up to you then to develop these skills so you are able to use them in your everyday life. As you begin to understand your talents or abilities, your FOCUS will begin to create what I like to think of as a new dimension. The world as we know it is two-dimensional and the laws that govern us in this world are clear. There are things you will and will not be able to do in this two-dimensional world. When your FOCUS starts living up to its true potential, it will create what I like to think of as a third dimension. This third dimension will give your talents, abilities and dreams an almost physical tangibility. It will almost feel like looking at the world through 3-D glasses. Your new awareness of everything will give your life a new positive direction. Like a 3-D picture, everything looks like you can reach out and touch it! That "Whole World" experience I spoke about earlier. Traditionally listening may not be considered a talent and it doesn't really make me a superhero, but I recognized it was given to me. I believe in it because I know my ability to listen does help people. I believe I should have been a therapist, psychologist, or a psychiatrist. I wear everything I do with pride and respect and I have to be proud of who I am, and I truly must respect all those that confide in me. My ability to listen helped me to be extremely successful in my personal life, law enforcement career and in the world of private security. Working in these two worlds, listening has become a key component in what I do. Never look to luck and when you find out what your ability or talents are work hard at developing them. I don't believe there's any such thing as luck. I was told by one of my college professors Thel Glasgock that, "THE HARDER YOU WORK THE LUCKIER YOU GET." Hard work creates opportunities and FOCUS allows you to see them!

The morning I stood and looked in the mirror and decided I was going to listen again, was a great day. I accepted it and I had a clear idea as to why I was here. Of all the things I like to do this was something I had to do, "Listen". FOCUS has purpose in your life and every day you live; remember you are here for a specific reason. If you look and listen long and hard enough you will find Enlightenment, or it will find you. As you grow older you will think more and more about your purpose in life. One day you'll ask yourself, whether your life is active and full of promise or mundane. In my use of the aforementioned word "mundane" I did not use that word in any way to knock down or discredit anyone's dreams, wishes, or aspirations, or lack thereof. I've found even those whom may be financially stable or wealthy, sometimes lead mundane lives. For me "mundane" comes from a place of being unfulfilled in the heart. I'm not saying these people are not fulfilled because of money; I just want everyone to think about the person they are and why they are here. Look for purpose in your life and doing more than just getting from day to day. I believe your heart's activity sprouts a giving spirit and a giving spirit will always lead you to purpose, but you have to be open to it, and most importantly you have to look beyond you. Because of free will, purpose is something you will have to determine for yourself. I'm not saying because you have buckets of money to give everything away, but what I am saying is, as you give from the heart, the spirit with which you give will put pep in your Soul Step. "Heart Smile" is a part of the warm feelings you get in your stomach, or your chests letting you know you've done something you were supposed to do. You don't do it for public recognition so always let your spirit be your guide. When you help others, it creates a positive flow in your life. As I listen, I have found this is what helps me not only keep my FOCUS, but it gives me my positive flow. I listen never to judge the person or the statements made in a negative way. I've learned over the years that sometimes people just need to hear themselves, talk out whatever the situation is. Again, talking to yourself does not mean you are crazy, it means you just need to hear it out loud. Sometimes your spirit needs to verbally hear what's going on to help you react appropriately. If you don't have any questions about what's going on around you or if you're not asking yourself "Why are you here?" then you need to rethink where you might be going.

The positive affirmations you make in the mirror are a directive to help you find **"CLARITY IN PURPOSE" (CIP) PURPOSE,** is a noun and is defined as: the reason for which something is done or created, or for which something exists. **CIP** is understanding the who, what, and why you are here. Why you exist in the Universe and how your path and journey is a major part of a "Universal Chain," that keeps us together.

Why are you here, or why do you exist? Looking at the definition of purpose, I believe I am doing what I was created to do therefore I exist to do that which I was created for. Becoming a writer has been a long journey in my mind and spirit, but learning to believe in myself, became extremely necessary. We are often the last to believe what others are able to sometimes see right away. CIP is that tool provided to us I believe by the Universe. I have seen it time and time again where someone because of circumstance, or bad environment, or any other negative situation are still able to become a doctor, a lawyer, a business owner or even the President of the United States. Your purpose will always lead you to success if you recognize how it works and allow it to work with you. Passion, drive and desire are three key components in understanding your purpose. The most important component of purpose is summed up by a quote from Montel Williams, "You are the only one who owns the definition of who you are!" This is a key component in finding and understanding your purpose.

As I look back at the career of basketball great Magic Johnson. I see a hall of fame basketball player who was truly blessed with what I believe was God given talent. He did things on the basketball court most of us could only dream of doing and even in our dreams we still couldn't manage to pull them off. Even though he had this God given talent one day he had to realize what he was given. Right? Knowing his abilities were far better than his peer's he didn't just rest on his laurels. He practiced and studied his craft from A to Z allowing his abilities to grow, develop and shine thus discovering his purpose. At 6 feet 9 inches, two hundred thirty-one pounds, Magic changed the face of what was considered a point guard in the NBA. Magic Johnson… the man, the myth, the legend! To be the player he became, he needed to have incredible FOCUS and a strong belief in himself that he could do whatever he wanted to with a basketball. Magic Johnson changed the game of basketball by recognizing what he could become and I have to believe he took advantage of every opportunity placed before him. You don't get to where Magic is without opportunities and recognizing they are for you.

Magic Johnson had to come to the realization he was placed here on Earth at that time to play basketball. He was voted one of the fifty best players in the NBA history. He also won Olympic gold with the "Dream Team." I use this example so you can see the success of an athlete pretty much everyone in the world recognizes. Even though Magic Johnson's basketball career was cut short by his announcement he contracted the Aids Virus, it didn't slow his pace or stop his FOCUS in any way. Magic owned the definition of who he is on and off the court! Again, Magic's example goes just a little further than basketball. To show the ultimate FOCUS, during Magic's basketball career, he's also become an extremely successful businessman, a true entrepreneur. His success in business has made him a force to be reckoned with and between his real estate investments and franchise ownership; Magic Johnson has proven that once you learn to FOCUS nothing is out of reach. Now why are "YOU" here?

I know what you're thinking… well, well, that's Magic Johnson. He's a basketball superstar! Yes, he is but he wasn't born the man he is today. He may have been born with the athletic ability but as he got older, he and others recognized it, so no matter how smart you are, or how athletic you are, if you don't put in the time to develop your abilities, it's wasted talent. The point I'm trying to drive home is, as you move forward in your life, you will continue to learn things about yourself. As you to learn, everything that's stored in your spirit will help you to fuel the machine that is your FOCUS. When opportunities come your way, you will always be ready, but you will also learn to recognize situations and be able to react to them without hesitation. Your "Unconscious Consciousness," is what will begin to take over when positive things happen in your life. I learned many things as a deputy sheriff and a police officer, but if I were not trained properly by the academy staff and if I didn't do any training on my own once I left the academy, I could have found myself in some life-threatening situations, that I may not have come out of. Whatever you do for a living, we all know training and experience is what allows you to grow. After a certain point our Unconscious Consciousness becomes our guide assisting in our success. When you begin to understand why you are here, your FOCUS will have great direction keeping you on the road to strength and power. Your strength will become more than just physical; your mental strength and attitude will become extremely important. Looking at the Magic Johnson example of a successful life is how I want you to start envisioning your life. Believe me it's not as hard as we make it. Mind you, anything worth doing is worth working for and that must be your mindset going in. Hard work is an absolute must, but having a plan is extremely necessary. Start developing a plan for your life that will force anyone looking in to see you and your purpose. If you work for someone let your co-workers and your boss or your immediate supervisor see that you are worth what they are paying you. If you are the owner of a company let your employees see you are someone they would devote their ninety-five percent talent to and the effort of the additional five percent, they will give to you without hesitation. We all have to learn to dedicate ourselves to our purpose in this life. What are you good at? What do you like to do that you can earn a living doing? Have you ever felt so strongly about something but were afraid to test the waters? Everyone has had these questions and then some. Having questions is good, but acting on them is better. I had questions for years about becoming a writer and I look at Unlikely Destiny Volume One, as my question answered. Don't ever stop asking yourself questions, but one day you're going to have to respond to them. As my life continues to grow day by day I am happy in the knowledge that, I will never stop learning about myself or learning from everyone I come in contact with. Every time I ask myself, why are you here? I can answer that question… "I AM A LISTENER BUT MOST OF ALL I AM A WRITER!"

As a writer, being able to reach into "THE CLARITIES" increased my FOCUS in writing, but recognizing CIP brought everything together for me. CIP helps you avoid many of the mistakes you would make in life because you have a clearer direction of the path you should be on. If you have some idea where you are going, this increases the opportunity for success in whatever it is you are meant to do. Being able to remember what I hear and read, gives me a great advantage as it allows me to write with a purpose and that's not only made me a much better writer, it's made me a much better person. Enough about me let's get back to you. Why are you here? You're here because you have a message for the world and, no matter how big or small you think this message is you need to find a way to get it out. When I say you have a message for the world that is strictly a metaphor, but I want you to believe in your spirit, your purpose in life is just that important. Your point of being as dramatic as it might sound is completely necessary in the balance of our Universe. Every single thing you do has purpose and every single thought you have, has specific meaning. You need to learn to believe that and as you think about the things you want to do, looking at the talents and abilities you were born with, should help you to understand, "WHY YOU ARE HERE." As you begin to understand why you are here the level of confidence you live your life with is going to change. The change will be extremely subtle at first, because you're not used to the new power, but as time passes you will get used to it and learn to accept this new confidence to reinforce your strength. Remember nothing happens overnight so you're going to have to learn patience. This level of confidence will begin to change your approach to every situation, allowing you the ability to expect opportunities and because you do expect, you learn to accept. Learning to trust yourself and the 3D images you will begin to see, that's when you will feel your FOCUS increasing.

Throughout this book I will refer to famous quotes, because I believe they really help you to get your point across. Quotes also help the reader to remember key points in what they have read. An Academy Award Winning actress has a quote I think is so appropriate for this chapter… "Nothing should be permanent except our struggle with the dark side within ourselves." Shirley MacLaine said this. I love this quote for, "Why Are You Here?" because as you begin to discover who you really are and what your true purpose is, it's going to create an internal struggle, like you've never experienced. I'm not trying to scare you I'm just getting you prepared for the challenges. "The struggle is real." Even though this struggle is tough to deal with, it helped me with the anger and depression, I spoke on earlier. It's a process, but it's also a part of our lives we need to learn from. Remember learning and challenges are there to increase your FOCUS and make you stronger. FOCUS will help you move forward, but a major part of the struggle will sometimes come from how you earn a living and what you are meant to do, to balance the universe and still earn that living. It's a tough situation, but the balance necessary to make them both work, can be earth shattering. You will struggle with this, as we all have when you try and make a life changing decision. I have known for so very long that I am a writer, but the struggle I wrestled with was earning a living. When I started, I learned all I could about writing and writers. At the time, I didn't think writers except for a few of the very good ones, earned a decent living as a writer. (Stephen King being one of my favorites) Again it's not about the money if it's your passion, but if you have responsibilities you still need to earn a living and there-in lies the internal struggle, and the pain of me not thinking I could do both. We all have to start somewhere. I always go back to the thoughts I had as a child and the dreams that were stored in my memories and I will always remember, I never give up on anything I believe is worth working for especially myself. Even though I was earning a living in law enforcement and private security I continued to write in my spare time. The passion to write is my medicine and my comfort. Because of the high stress levels in both jobs I have done for the past thirty plus years, writing just like long drives with a destination relax me. So, I wrote short stories and I practiced writing treatments for television shows, scripts for feature films, etc. You name it, I wrote it. I continued to work on my creative flow so to speak, because I knew one day I would sit down and write something that I could be truly proud of, even if no one else read what I had written. If I wrote a book and had to self-publish it and stand on street corners to sell it I would do so, because writing is and will always be my passion. Everything I could do that had to do with writing I did. I took writing classes, I also read and purchased books about writing. I had even been placed in the position to meet several writers (I wonder how that happens?) and I was able to ask them about their motivation to write certain pieces and about their writing style. I learned as much as I could everyday about writing, every aspect and every angle. Being able to do what I know I'm supposed to do makes me feel alive. Live for what you love to do and FOCUS will help you move to the next level. Opportunities continue to present themselves to me on a daily basis, because I am truly aware they exist. Part of the reason I did not write this book before was like I told you, FEAR! Fear of the unknown sets all of us up for failure every time. FOCUS takes that fear and stuffs it in a box allowing you to ship it away like a Fed Ex package. FOCUS also teaches you to use the fear that once slapped you upside the head, as a stepping-stone. We all have fears about doing something different. This is also the reason for our internal struggle, about doing something new. That's never going to change unless you change the way you approach every challenge. Fear is like most of the bullies that lived in your neighborhood growing up: if you learn to deal with fear in that one on one stage, it's not as scary and in most cases fear, like the bully, will back down. If you continue to let your fears pile up and become a gang, kind of like the "Compton Crips" this becomes a much harder situation to deal with. In most cases when it comes to fear I've discovered that the unknown scares most of us to death. That is probably why most of us fear death, because we don't know what happens after we die and in many cases it's not death, it's the way people die, that's the scary part. Okay enough about death let's get back to why we are here… to live!

I have to believe FOCUS has been in my spirit all of my life, but for the last fifteen years, it has manifested itself in me, in my cell phone and on my walls at home. From Opportunity Comes Unlimited Success is my FOCUS for the future and as I continue to learn to flex this muscle, it's getting so strong that I almost can't control it. That's a good thing because your, Unconscious Consciousness is a great way to live and it's a great way to see the world around you. It's like breathing, or your heart pumping blood to every area of your body, you don't have to think about it. Unconscious Consciousness, Joe the writer will continue to exist because he knows why he is here. I believed for a very long time I was a writer. I have always been a writer and I will always be a writer. I will continue to study my craft… did I just say my craft? Yes, I did! I have learned to accept my reason for being. Trying to figure out or understand why you are here should become a priority in your life. Seeing your FOCUS through clarity in vision could become so clear at some point, objects that were once large hurdles are like a step up onto a curb, not much effort needed there. The internal struggles will still be there, but your FOCUS will help you to pass through them and not allow them to hinder your forward progress. Self-doubt, insecurity, thoughts of being inadequate are always going to haunt you, we're human. Delete, delete, delete, the old way of responding to situations. You can't allow negative thoughts to take up residence in your spirit like they've done in the past. In chapter one I gave you a little background information on the environment I grew up in. I decided as I sat down to write this book I was going to space out my life story by placing a little bit of it in each chapter, of each book. I don't feel that a person's life can be summed up in one chapter, because as people we continue to grow and develop at different levels and even though this growth takes place the way it does, it never happens overnight. In trying to understand why we are here, you have to remember that life takes time and as time passes, hopefully we live and continue to learn. As long as you are alive taking up space in this Universe you must continue to learn. Keep in mind that in this learning process your FOCUS is also developing.

I spoke about my parents Joe and Josephine Pryor in chapter one. They are two of the people, along with both of my grandmothers, Pinkie Thomas and Susan Littlejohn, who raised me. I think they did a pretty good job laying the foundation for what made me who I am today. I have discovered one of the realities of life is, the people who raise you have good and bad qualities. I know you're thinking-not my parents! They are the best parents in the whole wide world. I'm not saying they are the worst thing in your life, I'm just saying that everyone has a thing or two in their lives they wish they could do over and some of these people happen to have raised us. I surely do and so should you! None of us are perfect and when you think you are, you'll find out if you're smart, you still have a lot to learn. The learning process should be a part of our daily lives. Another important part of our daily lives is free will, always floating around our environment. I still had to make choices and I think I chose the right road to travel most of the time. Even with the foundation laid by these four-amazing people, free will was always my choice to steer my life in what I thought was the right direction. Unknown to pretty much everyone, I grew up most of my childhood with such a chip on my shoulder, I am sometimes surprised I didn't take the wrong road more than I did. I was so good at hiding my feelings, that none of my friends were able to see the anger, I had living inside of me. I didn't want it there and I did my best to maintain control over it. The insecure child who didn't think he'd live to see his 30th birthday had a deep dark secret. The only person I ever expressed any of these feelings to at a young age was my friend Mickey. When I was eighteen, Mickey was killed and the chip on my shoulder grew even larger. As an adult I told no one because I thought it would make me appear weak. It eventually took over my spirit creating a very dark cloud. When I spoke of him in chapter one, I said he was like the brother I never had. There was so much anger living inside me during this time, even as I write these words I can feel anger swelling up inside me again. I am strong... I am focused... Nothing will ever stop me! I used to think and then say these words out loud to myself every day. I would find out later this is just one of the triggers lying dormant in my spirit trying to act out.

LIFEWORK JOURNAL ENTRY

I was told at a very young age my biological mother, the woman who gave birth to me, didn't want me. Several members of my family told me this and as a young child we have a tendency to believe what is put into our spirits creating negative memories. It doesn't matter who said it, this is what I believe created the first negative chip on my shoulder. I knew the mother who raised me was my step-mom and believe me she did an amazing job. First of all, the fact that she loved me without question became a driving force in my life. Someone loving me just because, man I did everything I could to be the good son. Even though I harbored anger in my heart about so many things, there was still a large amount of love for the things I could see. On the other side of the coin I believed deep, deep, deep in my heart at times love couldn't exist because my "MOTHER" didn't love me! The mother who had given birth to me was not in my life and I believed she didn't want me! This is where internally I became an angry black child. As you grow and mature and look back at your life, (Clarity in Memory) you will be able to see in many cases the when, where, why, what and how's, of your life. What made you change for the good or bad in your life? I chose to be angry with someone I didn't even know. I chose to have preconceived ideas about someone without having all the facts. At this point in my life I had not discovered clarity in others: which was really a reflection of me at the time trying to figure out why I was here. When you feel unwanted on any level you begin to question the point of your existence. As a deputy sheriff and a police officer I always made arrest based on facts and evidence, not hearsay or conjecture. As a child I didn't know any better, so I believed what I was told. It is a true blessing that we are able to live and learn.

PAUSE LIFEWORK JOURNAL ENTRY

Believe it or not the anger I experienced back then is what I believe sparked the beginning of FOCUS in my life. I know FOCUS also saved my life and kept me on a pretty straight path. FOCUS made me study in school so I could acquire the knowledge I needed to be successful. During that time the negative side of my FOCUS was to be a success so my "MOM" would see me one day and wish she had been in my life. "I'll show her!" I said to myself. "She didn't want me so I didn't want her!" I thought to myself on a daily basis. Yeah right… I don't care who you are, or where you came from, you want to know who you are and you want to know whom your parents are. I think people who say they don't care who their parent is, are not being honest with themselves. Even as you acquire what you think is success you will still feel the void or the missing pieces to your puzzle and trust me it will haunt you to no end. It's my feeling, "You are the sum total of all the things you have been through and survived." These situations shape your character and because you survived them you need to realize you have point and purpose in this Universe, beyond any circumstance.

LIFEWORK JOURNAL CONTINUED

On October 1st 1993 I moved to New York, leaving the Inglewood Police Department, starting my security company and working full time for Montel Williams and the Montel Williams Show. What an amazing opportunity for me. I didn't really want to leave the west coast but since I have always had a spirit of adventure, I packed my bags and took to the road. Moving to New York was quite an adjustment, but I have learned to work in this fast-paced world without losing myself. I'm still Joe from the Westside. I was in my apartment one day and my telephone rang. There was a woman (who I later found out was my sister Debbe) on the other end of the phone, who said she was calling from California and she also said she was my sister and wanted to meet me. I was completely shocked and speechless. Mind you I'm 33 years old and someone claiming to be my sister wants to meet me. The anger I thought had been under control turned immediately to "RAGE!" I was so angry I could feel my entire body starting to get hot like I was in a microwave oven. From the inside out I started to shake with unfocused anger. Why was I so mad? To this day I could not tell you why, but here I am Mr. "Big Time Listener" and I didn't want to hear what my sister, my blood who reached out to me, had to say. I don't even remember saying good-bye before I hung up the phone. Who did I think I was? Joe Pryor angry black man, that's who! Later I would have to eat every word I shouted at her in anger. That sucked! But eat them I did. Clarity in Memory helps to keep me learning. Sometimes we have to remember so we can move forward in life to the positive. The biggest lesson I learned from this situation is always listen to everything, remain calm and don't lose your FOCUS.

One day (three years later) I decided to call one of my cousins and made inquiries about my biological mother. My cousin (Evette Darty) told me that she knew my sister. "Her name is Debbe," she said. She said she would call me back later in the week with her phone number. I spoke with my cousin on a Tuesday and she called me back on Friday of the same week and gave me Debbe's phone number. I remember the multitude of feelings running through my spirit. I was still extremely angry and afraid, but the fear that drove me away from listening three years earlier, gave me the ability to hear this time. I was truly a mess! Big step, "do I call or just let it go?" I made the call… as the phone rang I remember so badly wanting to hang up, but I didn't. Debbe, finally picked up the phone after several rings;

> I said, "Hello, can I speak to Debbe?"
> "This is Debbe, who's calling?"
> "This is Joe…Joe Pryor"
> "Is this, Joe Pryor?"
> "Yes, it is."
> "Joe Pryor, Joe Pryor?"
> "Yes"
> "SILENCE!"

After I said, "Yes" there was complete silence on the other end of the phone. It seemed like we were silent for about an hour, but it was only seconds. I could feel my heart beating out of my chest and in my throat.

END LIFEWORK JOURNAL ENTRY

That's pretty much how our initial conversation started with my sister Debbe. She was also the same person who had reached out to me in 1993. Debbe along with my other sister Mara (who was on the other line of a three-way call at the time) had also heard and felt my anger in our first conversation in 1993. Debbe went on to tell me Mara was hurt by my words and might not want to speak with me anytime soon. But she was very happy I had called her. Remember what I said about watching what you say? Words spoken from your spirit in anger are an extremely powerful tool. They cut the person you throw them at, but these words will eventually cut you too. I'm still nursing those wounds. We spoke for over an hour and I told her I was coming to Los Angeles later in the week and would like to meet with her. She agreed, so when I arrived in Los Angeles I was still angry about what I believed was the truth and I was trying to find every excuse to back out of our meeting. I remember asking her not to tell anyone I was coming out there because I just wanted to meet with her and if things went well, I would eventually meet my mom and the rest of my siblings, at another time. I decided to go to her house shortly after I arrived in Los Angeles. At the time, Debbe lived in the city of Hawthorne California and the city of Hawthorne borders the city of Inglewood's south side. Remember I worked for the Inglewood Police Department for several years. Debbe lived on a street named Kornblum Avenue near the 105 freeways in Hawthorne California. When Debbie told me, she lived on Kornblum Avenue, near the 105 freeways I knew exactly where it was, because I used to sit in my police car and write my reports on her street, literally across from her house. I had no idea she lived in that house and I continually find it amazing how small the world is. A couple of times over the years as I sat in my police car, I remember seeing Debbe leave her house. I get a chill every time I think about how close she was to me and as I write this, it almost brings tears to my eyes. I will continue to believe; things happen in your life the way they are supposed to. I believe in one way or another we would have met, but it just happened the way it was supposed to at that time. I think about now how funny it would have been, if she had ever walked over to my patrol car and looked at the nametag on my chest… that would have been something to talk about? I met with Debbe and I shared with her I had seen her several times while working for Inglewood PD, parked outside of her house. From that point Focus Forward, we connected! We talked for a couple of hours. As you make this journey in search of yourself, understand everything you may go through and all that you experience is creating your soul step. Live it, learn to love it and yourself, but most importantly think about "Why are you here?" Yes, I did meet my biological mother. Everyone I know has said this at one point in their lives about having something extremely difficult to do. We have all been there, haven't we? When I say this was difficult it's an understatement! "At that point in my life this was by far the hardest thing I have ever had to do, and here's why: I was going to have to sit in a room with a woman who I had never met, my biological mother, and listen to her objectively, without losing it and hear every word from her and do it with an open heart." Are you following me? You want to talk about stress!!! Working for The Montel Williams Show in the 1990's we were known for doing our share of reunion shows. Reuniting lost loves, bringing brothers and sister together, and my favorite, putting parents back together with their children. Every time we did one of these shows, I wondered how my meeting with my mom would be? When my mother arrived at my sister Debbe's house she gave me a hug and I could feel her body tremble, but her hug felt genuine. I was used to people being intimidated by my size, but I hoped this was not causing my mom to be afraid of me. She slowly sat down, looking at my face from top to bottom and side-to-side, then she looked me straight in the eye and proceeded to tell me what had happened. I have to say my mother never, not once, turned away from me while she spoke with me. I was doing what I do best… I was being the listener I was placed here to be. My mother was sitting in front of me pouring her heart out and right in the middle of her speaking with me I had an epiphany, every story of every person I had ever listened to, was preparing me for this moment. My heart was open and my spirit was filled to the brim with forgiveness, obedience, compassion understanding strength, with a spoon full of love, and patience, but most of all, a sense of who I really was. There was so much of her in me. We liked many of the same thing especially our taste in food, movies, T.V. shows, but most of all letting people know when we liked them and when we didn't. What I also learned that day is, everyone needs and deserves a second chance period! What you do with that second chance is up to you. I was given the ultimate second chance and I vowed to make the best of every second. Again, listening to her and not attacking her with my anger was the most difficult thing I have ever done. After it was all over and I had time to reflect, I was extremely proud of myself and even more proud of the fact I didn't allow fear to beat me this time! I used my fear as a stepping-stone to improve my life, which allows me to improve the lives of everyone I come into contact with. After we spoke, a couple of hours later, I realize the information I was given before I met her was completely false. I noticed something about my mother as I spoke with her; She looked me in the eye the entire time we spoke. I felt as if she was allowing me to look directly into her spirit, so I could see who she really was. She had been through a lot in her life, and I believe this is why she was able to look me in the eye. I also believed as she looked into my soul having nothing to hide, I learned something else extremely important that day. My good friend Lloyd McCullough always says, every story has three sides; "Your side, their side, and the truth that lies somewhere in the middle." Clarity in Others will always allow you to see the person not the situation. Looking for truth, as you should in every situation, allowed my mother and I to develop a beautiful relationship and I can say my mother's love is true and genuine. "It feels great to finally have her love." I've discovered even if there are pieces missing to your puzzle; it doesn't mean you can't see a complete picture. Filling in the blanks will become necessary at some point and FOCUS will also help you keep the right mental attitude so when adversity hits, you can hit back with confidence, courage and strength, going into every situation.

Are you thinking about why you are here? In the grand scheme of life missing pieces don't mean you fail, it only means you have to work a little harder to reach your goals. As I look at the spirit with which I live my life, I have learned many things. Remember, learning is always in effect. I've learned something about myself, I have never said out loud. I've been told by a very good friend, Amy Acton, that I have the patience of "Job" from the Bible. She also nicknamed me "The Saint" because of that patience. My patience developed mainly because I hate saying I'm sorry. There I said it! The main thing I've learned about being a listener, my patience has been tested and during those tests, I've found cooler heads always prevail. Case and point, because I allowed myself to be angry about the situation with my mother, I lost it the first time I spoke with my sister Debbe and when I called her three years later to inquire about my mother, I had to chew on every angry word I spit at her and my sister Mara. When I realized Debbe was the sister I had spoken to in anger, I immediately apologized. As I said earlier, I hate apologizing, but I will always do it when I screw up. I have to do the right thing and if I'm wrong, I will admit it, to keep my life and the life of someone I may have offended moving Focus Forward. Not getting angry or upset allows you to think through situations and this will always allow you to see every side of what's going on, so you can make a sound decision each and every time. As you look at yourself and think about why you are here, the clearer your thoughts, the more FOCUS you will have in your thinking. You'll see opportunities again and again and know they are there for you. Keeping in mind, as you think so shall you be. As you begin understanding "YOU", you will see so many sides to yourself and in those sides, you must allow the positive to flow. Allowing the positive to flow means not beating yourself up when you make a decision that does not work out the way you intended. "NO" will always mean "NEXT OPTION" time. Making the decision to meet my mother and my eight other siblings was extremely tough, but I made it and I know for a fact I am a much better person for it. I have an amazing relationship with my Mom and to this day I believe meeting her has helped me in every area of my life. Personally, it's made me a better person and I know I'm a better man. Both Debbe and Mara have forgiven me and we have moved on to have an amazing relationship. I have also been to several family reunions and I have developed relationships with my other brothers and sisters. Not ever relationship is going to be perfect, but as long as you contribute from your heart, that's all you can do. Clarity in Memory will never let me completely forget my feelings that day, but the knowledge I've gained from this experience has truly been life changing. The longer you dwell on negative situation, the longer your life will be out of FOCUS. Every explorer that left their land, going out to find a new world, was in many cases looking for themselves and they were also fulfilling their purpose. Pushing yourself will give you additional insight into who you can become. It will also give you the ability to "Think outside the box." (I will talk more about "Thinking Outside the Box" in chapter five). As you explore discovering "YOU," you will see your life is going to go through many changes. You will not only learn about yourself, you will learn about your family, friends, co-workers and even strangers. Opening yourself up to the clarities, in thought, vision, memory, others and purpose, will give you the extra-added confidence to keep your soul step operating at a high level. Learning to listen the first time, you will begin to trust yourself and, in most cases, trusting your first mind is the best option.

I decided to tell the story about meeting my mother and of course my siblings, because even though there was a great foundation laid by my parents and grandmother's, I had developed a hairline crack that was beginning to grow each year clouding my FOCUS. CIP allowed me to see beyond the circumstance I found myself placed in. Even though I was using negative motivation to stay on track, I was still able to develop FOCUS but how long could I keep this up. My purpose to win at life, surviving the neighborhoods, learning to see beyond my circumstances, grew to become my strength. It's funny even though I was told my mother didn't want me, I can only remember saying that out loud only one time in anger. I guess I didn't want that negative memory to take root in my spirit any more than it did. What we put in to everything is what we get back!

Initially I didn't tell my parents I had met and developed a relationship with my mother. When I finally decided to tell them, my step-mom got upset and began crying. I let my step-mom know it had nothing to do with her and everything to do with me. Then I advised the both of them to look at how I had turned out: I had never been to jail, but I did work there for a short time, I had never been arrested for anything, but I have arrested a lot of extremely bad people, I never joined a gang even though several of my friends had, because I had real love at home! I don't smoke anything, I didn't drink until I was forty-seven years old and that's only a little wine from time to time and I've never done drugs so please stop crying! Meeting my mother was about healing my heart in order to become a better person. I needed to let go of the anger that created the negative chip in my armor and on my shoulder, that didn't allow me to enjoy my life. I needed to forgive in order to forgive myself. Before meeting my mother and speaking with her I thought she didn't want me because of who I was. I thought there was something wrong with me and that's what I fought with deep in my spirit every day! My mom finally calmed down, then the three of us sat and talked for a couple of hours about how I was doing with everything. When we finished what was the second toughest conversation of my life, I think they understood this was my journey and I needed to do it alone. There are going to be times in our lives that we need to complete a mission or two alone and everyone in your life is going to have to understand.

LIFEWORK JOURNAL ENTRY

I was trying to explain the basic concept of Unlikely Destiny, specifically "Why Are You Here" to a co-worker and how everyone has a point and purpose in life. She wasn't buying what I was selling even with my money. I decided to break it down this way… I told her it was my belief that most of us don't know why we are here and specifically we all have the ability for greatness on some level, large and small. You could do something as simple as saying hello to someone, changing their day to make it just a little better or you could have a child who could do something great without even trying. A split second in time could be the difference in changing the world or your environment. She listened, but I really don't think she was too receptive to it. A little later that afternoon she found herself walking from the office to run an errand. As she crossed the street at Fifty-fourth Street at Ninth Avenue in New York City, she began to cross the street against the red light, texting one of her clients. Now halfway in the street she looks up, as a taxicab is about to hit her, she panics and stops right there in the street. Just as the taxicab was about to strike her, a man grabbed the back of her coat pulling her out of the way of the taxicab, possibly saving her life. She said the man never stopped. He just saved her life and kept walking like it was no big deal. She said she saw her life leave her body and nearly passed out. She began to cry as she looked for the person who had just saved her, but lost him in the crowd. I could see that she had been crying, so I said to her this person was at this exact spot, at this exact time, for one reason and one reason only, Clarity in Purpose. This is one of the reasons he was born, to be at that intersection, so you could live to see another day. I asked her, "Now that have another chance at life, what are you going to do? She said, "I have a lot to think about!" You need to ask yourself, "WHY ARE YOU HERE"? As simple as that sounds I believe that's how our Universe works.

END LIFEWORK JOURNAL ENTRY

I would like to share another "Matrix Moment" with you. If you didn't see the Matrix Trilogy, the Morpheus character's whole purpose and existence became "FINDING THE ONE", who happened to be Neo.

He never lost "FAITH" or "FOCUS" in the fact that his entire life and purpose is based on finding the person who was going to save mankind. Morpheus never wavered from his mission and even though The Matrix is just a movie, that's the mindset you need to have when you discover why you are here. That discovery will lead you down a road giving your purpose more internal credibility to keep your life on the right track to achieve your goals. If a child has a knack for solving complex math equations or another who understands science better than his or her teacher, either their parents, a teacher or a self-appointed mentor, given by the Universe, will recognize this child's ability, help them with FOCUS to cultivate their skill or purpose bringing it to fruition. Everyone you meet, you have to know they have been place before you to help you on your journey. Everything we are placed here to do is not to impress the masses or even a single person. If you use your abilities for selfish reason they will never develop fully and we lose balance in our personal environment and the Universe. This ability has been given to you for a specific reason and trying to ignore "IT"," doesn't make "IT" go away. Look at what happened to me when I decided to stop listening. The bigger picture of why we are all here is to help each other understand our existence, because we can't do any of this alone.

As I stand here back in the mirror, my FOCUS is at a medium glow growing and moving toward full, strengthening my soul step every single day. My attitude has been adjusted and leaning always toward the positive side of my life. I need you to ask yourself again, "Why Are You Here?" Moving Focus Forward, "Knowing What You Want" will only increase your ability to succeed...

4

What Do You Want?

A winner is someone who recognizes his God given talents works his tail off to develop them into skills and uses these skills to accomplish his goals...

Larry Bird

How many times have you been asked the question: "What do you want"? As children we are asked this question repeatedly by our parents, brothers and sisters, teachers and many times by our friends. It's funny because as children we pretty much know exactly what we want and we will ask for whatever is on our minds, because we don't understand limitations or the word "NO." As time passes and we begin living our lives, several words and ideas develop in our vocabulary, finding their way deep, down into our spirit causing our SOUL STEP to miss a step or two: REJECTION, FEAR, UNCERTAINITY, DOUBT, INSECURITY, A LACK OF BELIEF IN OUR ABILITIES and of course the word "NO!" They begin eating away at our spirit causing us to lose FOCUS. Knowing what you want on every level is more than half the battle. As we get older mainly because there is so much going on in our lives, we lose sight of what we want. Often times we let the life we've created get in the way of our dreams, causing us to sometimes lose our passion, drive and desire. The Larry Bird quote at the beginning of this chapter is key because it tells me we need to set goals in order to know or have an idea as to what we want! I've known for a very long time what I wanted. I wanted to be a writer. "WRITER" was buried deep inside my spirit waiting for me to develop. Yes, I said waiting for me to develop, because rejection and fear continued clouding my judgment. I spoke earlier about being born with certain abilities and recognizing what you have. Cultivating what you've been given is the work you'll have to put in because this is key in your development. Even though writing was in my spirit, once I recognized it, I had to let it out. I told you I took classes and read books, but most of all I used practical application exercises by writing. One of the best things about knowing what you want, it allows you the opportunity to FOCUS your energy in a specific direction, on a specific idea, but most importantly on the dreams buried in your spirit. I know I talk about spirit a lot, but I believe everything that is "YOU" are coded in there like a computer's hard drive. Every ability given to you at birth is coded in your DNA, on your internal hard drive, developing inside you, waiting to be accessed. If you think about what you want, linked many times with your abilities you have to think about how that plays out in the Universe. Thoughts and ideas have to come from someplace deeper than your brain. More than what is on the surface drives us and you have to believe that on some level. The passion that flows through your veins is not some random feeling you get for no reason. Everything you do is from a desire and as a belief deep down inside you can do anything. What do you want?

Passion, Drive and Desire also known, as PDD will be referred to in this chapter over and over again. I want you to understand all three of these words, so we are going to look at them individually and then we'll put them together. Most of us think we know these words because we may use them every day, but because we may use them so often my belief is words sometimes lose their true meaning or they get lost in our translation of them. When words lose their meaning we sometimes live our lives according to the way we use or live them. And since we sometimes use them incorrectly we live our lives in the same manner. Let's start by living with and looking at the word Passion.

Passion is a noun and it is defined as:
1) Intense or overpowering emotion such as love, joy, hatred, or anger.
2) Strong sexual desire and excitement.

Let's take a look at Drive. Since I like high performance or muscle cars, when I think about drive I like pushing it to the limit while maintaining complete control.

Drive is a verb and it is defined as:
1) To supply the power that makes something work.
2) To provide momentum toward the successful operation or functioning of something.

Desire really doesn't need any definition or does it? Desire as a word that gets straight to the point.

Desire is a verb and it is defined as:
1) To want something very strongly.
2) To wish for and request something.
3) A wish, craving, or longing for something.

Each of these words has several definitions, but in each case, of each word these are the definitions I chose to use. These definitions I believe will help me to help you understand the PDD Factor in this chapter and how PDD has helped to really change the way I look at my life and how I approach my day, every day I wake up. Each one of these words by themselves is powerful, but joined together; you are armed with three of the most powerful words in our Unlikely Destiny arsenal. If you learn to believe in them as I do, they will take you places you never thought you could go! Let me explain how...

I opened this chapter with a quote from Larry Bird, which I hope you read a couple of times. Get it down deep into your spirit and remember what I said about quotes, "they help us to remember things or points in our lives," but what I haven't told you is these quotes in many cases help to give our lives meaning. Getting back to Larry he said "A winner is someone who recognizes his God given talents works his tail off to develop them into skills and uses these skills to accomplish his goals!" You should never forget this as long as you live, because this is going to be the new definition of your life. If Larry Bird doesn't equal PDD then you can stop reading right now. You know he does so don't even think about closing this book… FOCUS!

I like the beginning of Larry's quote because he separates himself from the rest of the competition by establishing himself as a winner. "A winner is someone who recognizes his God given talents." I also look at this quote and it reminds me there are winners and losers. I look at losing as an unfocused ball of confusion, that most of us have found ourselves rolled up into at one time or another. Unprepared in your intent and lacking in the knowledge of your purpose is not Focus Forward living. This truly sounds like a lot of mumbo jumbo, but breaking it down is just another way of saying you need to study to show yourself approved. Gathering the knowledge about what it is you want to do is one of the first steps when you decide, what it is you want. Losing does not mean you are a loser. We have all lost at something in our lives more times than we have won and it's ok as long as you don't ever stop trying to succeed, at whatever it is you wish to accomplish. Like I said earlier, losing is something that happens when you are unprepared and not ready for the task at hand, but being a loser can become a state of mind or a point of being. There are going to be times when you are prepared and you still may not accomplish your goals. Don't let that discourage you because, Joel Osteen has a quote that I Love in this situation: "Each set back is a set up for something better." Your accomplishments are always marked by visible success, but in order to achieve that success, you had to try at some point and fail! Failing doesn't mean you lose, it just means "NEXT OPTION." Knowing what you want helps you exercise your mind in the right direction allowing you to keep your eye on the prize, in a manner of speaking.

One of the best things about knowing I wanted to be a writer is it cuts down on any wasted time I would otherwise go through if I didn't know. This will also help your FOCUS to develop faster, because you are not trying to figure out why you are doing certain things. As I look back over my life my FOCUS has greatly influenced me, and the lives of the people around me. Listening and giving advice to those I love and care about not only helps them, but it helps me in ways that continue to make my heart smile. The key to all of this is helping others to do their best. When you help people with an open heart it not only helps to develop your FOCUS, but it continues to develop you as an individual. As a listener, knowing it was the gift I was given, I will always be thankful for that knowledge. I know what I am here to do (LISTEN) and I know what I want to do, (WRITE) but I also believe my ability to write is another extremely precious gift and it also has to be done.

Passion, Drive and Desire are three words that are now a part of your life and you can't give them back. I say it that way because "Once you learn anything no one can take it away from you." Knowledge can be dangerous only because once you have it you will become the Passion that creates the Drive, leading you to understanding the Desires of your life and your heart. I can't imagine my life without PDD because it has given me the ability, to grow into the person I am today. I've learned that anything done with minimal effort will give you minimal or no return. If you are not going to give 100% with everything you do, you are wasting time in your life and everyone you come in contact with. If you choose not to give 100% in your relationships, or if you decide not to give 100% in your job, or if you choose not to give your children 100% of your full attention, when they ask you a question, then you will get back what you put in. It's a part of why I am here to help, but I also want to pass on my ability to listen.

Let's say for example you want to become a doctor? As early as you can remember you wanted to be a doctor so you've decided your mission in life is to help heal the sick and or take care of those less fortunate physically than most. Where do you think your desire came from? Since you know you want to do this you have to learn to start shifting your FOCUS in the direction of being a doctor. Being a doctor takes a world of FOCUS and an equal amount of work. Once you've decided on this course of study where does your PDD factor in all of this? Do you have the PDD to be a doctor? You have heard me speak early on about the "Soul Step" and what it means in the development of your FOCUS. What is it? Your Soul Step is always going to be your confidence and it comes directly from your spirit. Not arrogance, its confidence! The confidence of knowing you did your homework on whatever it is you needed to study. The confidence you know; you were born to do this! It is also a point of reference you will come to feel every day you wake up. I am not a morning person. I am a nocturnal, meaning I am a modern-day vampire. I am like the comic book character "Blade." A day walker of sorts… I believe because I was born at 12:43 a.m. I like being awake at night; so late nights' equal slow mornings. Even though my mornings are slow I have learned to embrace and be thankful in each day especially the mornings. The quiet of every morning allows the clarity in my spirit, to be re-enforced. As I wake up each morning, the reflective mirror in my spirit, allows me to see a clearer picture of my life in my mind and this also helps to re-enforce my Soul Step.

Now I need for you to do me a favor… KEEP IT ALL A SECRET! Don't tell anyone what it is you want to do. And you're thinking why would I do that? I take this life-long journey, on this impossible quest for fire and I can't tell anyone? I mean I finally decide what it is I want to do with my life and it's got to remain a "SECRET?" Yeah that's pretty much how it goes. I hate to make it sound so cold, but that's how it is and here's why. As you begin to become enlightened and a new way of thinking and living your life starts to rear its ugly head, (LOL) the new creation you are becoming, won't be understood by most of the people that are a part of your life. I'm not saying everyone will see the new you and not be happy with it, just a select few. There will be times when the people around you won't understand the readjustments you have made. They won't understand your positive mindset or the PDD that has infected your attitude. Most of us are resistant to change. Even in small subtle doses we resist the changes in our everyday lives. Let me tell you when you start displaying your new, "I CAN DO THIS SPIRIT" to the positive, most people and I hate to say this, but often times it's the ones closest to us who will be the most resistant. When I say resistant it's just another way of saying the "N" Word.

Negative is a noun and is defined as:
1) Meaning No, or refusing or denying something.
2) Unhappy, discouraging, angry or otherwise detracting from a happy situation.
3) Pessimistic or tending to have a pessimistic outlook.

That's enough about the "N" Word! I don't like talking or writing about it, but I wanted you to have a part of the "N" word's true meaning. When I looked up the definition of negative, it was broken down into 12 different definitions. On the flip side, the word "POSITIVE" has 23 definitions. And the winner is POSITIVE!

Positive is a noun and is defined as:
1) Consisting in or characterized by the presence or possession of features or qualities rather than their absence.
2) With no possibility of doubt, clear and definite.

Positive can only win if you learn to FOCUS on it. Positive's definitions can only be useful or work for you when you recognize they exist and exercise your right to use them. Remember "Free Will", meaning everything is up to you.

If you stop and reflect about the people and events that are a part of your life, you will begin to see and truly understand why you are, where you are today. You will see successes and mishaps have occurred in your life and they can in many cases take you back to where you may have made a wrong turn. As you retrace your steps this should give you the opportunity to change the outcome of future situations because you have taken a look at your history. You may even be able to plot how and where the "N" Word entered your life affecting the promise of your life's daily successes and your overall happiness. Let's get back to why you keep things to yourself or as I said before, "Keeping The Secret." I skimmed the surface of the things I have been involved in over the years in Chapter 1. As I reflect about my own life in business, I have had great success, but I have had many if not more failures. One of the things I have learned from all of this is you never give up. I have also learned that failing at something does not make you a failure or a loser. Everything you experience creates growth if you allow it, but you have to be open and able to see it. I have also learned the more people you tell what you are doing, the more pressure you put on yourself to complete your task to meet their approval, or expectations. Remember none of what you do with your life should be done to impress anyone. The "N" word exists and most people live in this part of the world, not by choice but mostly by habit and condition. You don't anymore! Keep walking to the light and don't look back. PDD is your new constant state of being.

You need to know the space you occupy in this Universe should never be wasted. Every hour of every day should be filled with focused energy in the right direction. As you find your FOCUS and it continues to grow and develop, you will begin to see with clarity and understanding. As you gain perspective in knowing what you want, you will not only be able to see your goals, you will be able to achieve them without question. You have so many options in this life and you need to remember, they are right there in front of you every day.

Focus Forward in life is not only the right direction for you; it's the only direction you should choose. Let's take another look at free will. If you have a choice why not choose the positive? When you begin setting goals for what you want, self-doubt is going to knock on your Soul Step and when it does, learn not to answer the door. Listen, if you're at home, or your office or any place that has a door do me a favor, go over and open the door. When the door is open you can choose to stand in front of it and look at what's on the other side, or you can choose to walk through it and experience what's on the other side, or you can just close it. I say when you feel the slightest bit of the "N" word creeping up to the door, in this instance, just close the damn door! I want you to see that your free, will allows you to do either or. If you have been living a negative life and not chasing or trying to achieve your goals the way you should, you're selling yourself short, by not living your life the way it is meant to be. "Free Will" is our biggest blessing (Or possibly our biggest curse). It allows us to do what we choose, when we choose. What do you want? Free will gives you the opportunity to forgive. It allows you an obedience in certain situations. Free will lets you show compassion when your heart so pleases. It can take your understanding of every situation to a new level. It could also grant you the strength to make the right decisions for "YOU" when you are faced with a situation where you may have to stand-alone! What do you want?

What did I say earlier about keeping your goals to yourself? I said this because of human nature and the fact that most people really don't want to see anyone doing better than they are. It's sad and it sucks but this is a reality. Most people don't mean to be the way they are, it's just our competitive nature as humans to be successful. Case and point... when you tell someone you are working on a project and this project could be something major or minor, I've learned over the years anything worth doing never happens overnight. Trust me it took a while to write this book and most people I know had no idea I was working on it. Let's say you're at a dinner party and you tell several people during a conversation what you are working on. Out of the ten people you tell, four don't care, and three weren't really listening, because your Soul Step (confidence) was mistaken as bragging. The last three that did listen, only listened so every time they see you they make it a point to ask you about the project and in most cases their tone is masked with the "N" word. Of course, you begin to feel pressure every time you see these three people and it really sucks, because maybe you work with them, or they could be people you see, at least four or five days a week. Now out of those three-people asking you… "Hey, what's up with your project?" Only one of them truly has your best interest at heart. I know it would appear as though I'm throwing the "N" word around, right? I'm just looking at human nature and how people are. Competition in this society pushes us to do better than the next person and it also drives us in some cases to want to see others fail. Remember what I said about winners and losers, because in most cases you will fail more times than you'll win. You will have to stay focused during the tough times. Another way to keep your FOCUS is to not take anything personal when it comes to the negative people around you, or if your projects are rejected. If you spend time taking what these people say or do to heart, it will distract you from the goals you've set when a project doesn't come together, as quickly as you wished. The sooner you can delete the negative the sooner you can get back on track, "NEXT OPTION!" Don't allow yourself to get caught up in a self-pity party. Recognizing your God given talents is a part of the first steps you take in knowing what you want. Keeping in mind you still have to work your tail off, to get to a better understanding of whom you are and what it is you have to offer. Because I haven't asked in a while… "What do you want?" There has to be an idea floating around in your spirit, sparking your Soul Step right about now. I have an idea, don't stop reading; remember you took the red pill. I'm only reminding you of the choice you made to read this book. The strength in this chapter comes from you! The mindset in the Soul Step you have developed is yours to shape because you are in charge. The Enlightenment causing your spirit to open happens when you begin to understand who you really are and what you really want. Enlightenment more so than empowerment, is self-developed and not given to you by anyone. As we look at the words Empower and Enlightenment I want you to make the "CHOICE" as to where you'd like to stand, in understanding your development.

Empower is a verb and it is defined as:
1)   To give somebody power or authority (often passive)
2)   To give somebody a sense of confidence or self-esteem

Enlightenment is a noun and it is defined as:
1)   The enlightening of somebody or a cause of the enlightening of somebody.
2)   The condition of somebody who has been enlightened.

I'm not trying to take anything away from the word "empower" and I know for many people it has a place in their lives giving them a sense of strength and I think it's great but Enlightenment… gives me the sense as a person, I have grown because of the experiences I have survived and this growth allows me the opportunity to see the world with more clarity. As we become enlightened on every level we get the warm fuzzies in the pit of our stomachs and it lets you know you are on the right track. It also lets us know we have made another discovery about ourselves. The people we love, the world we live in and the Universe we occupy space in, we affect it every day. You have to decide how you want to affect the Universe. Enlightenment will become the shining light directing you down a clear path giving you the strength necessary to maneuver around or through any obstacles or challenges. Keeping what you want a secret is one of the best ways to keep the obstacles and challenges in your life to a minimum. Again, the people closest to us could in most cases be the ones creating most of the obstacles and challenges in our lives. Because of that I'm going to beg, no I'm going to demand if you know what's good for you to keep your mouth shut! As time passes you will learn who is truly happy for you and the goals you set. These people will have your back even if you decide you want to be the first pregnant man. I'm a little overboard, but your dreams and goals should be extreme. You should always reach for the moon and if you land amongst the stars that's not a bad place to be, plus you are still a lot closer to the moon now.

Another key component I've come to discover about my FOCUS is the less clutter I have the easier and more frequently my FOCUS flows. I know you're thinking… Wow, what a profound statement he just made. As simple as it sounds we have a tendency to complicate even the simple by allowing clutter to rule our lives. You put the clutter there so you're responsible for removing it. We will discuss more about your clutter and how to remove it in Chapter 5 Thinking outside the box. One of the best ways to get rid of clutter is to fill your box with the five clarities. (Clarity in THOUGHT, Clarity in VISION, Clarity in MEMORY, Clarity in OTHERS and Clarity in PURPOSE) Seeing your world and the world of the people around you will create a way for you to see each side of life's puzzle and not just your own pieces. I will let you in on another secret... negative can't survive in a "BOX" filled with Clarity.

In your everyday existence you should always try to see every point of view. I want you to take a minute or two and think about what you just read. Now that you're back let me try and explain what I mean by saying… "You never know what kind of day someone else is having." I use this example because unless you live in an ice cave all alone, you will have to come in contact with people every day. Everyone deals with and handles stress in different ways. Some people live for the stress their daily life dishes out and others die because of the same level of stress. All I'm saying is remember when you enter the world and that means, every day you wake up and leave your house, from this day Focus Forward, just remember one simple rule, "Treat everyone the way you want to be treated," all day, every day! The energy you put out will come back to you with the same level of force. I know I have told you this before, but as your FOCUS sharpens you will begin to read the people around you. Learning to see the people you meet and learning to understand them, believe it or not will aid you in finding out what you want. This also means you truly have to pay attention to the person next to you. You can't do anything alone and at some point, you're going to find that out, but when you decide to let people into your world bring the positive ones in. From time to time a negative person will slip through but it's okay because you can always remove them. (YOUR BOX, YOUR RULES!) You will start to see and feel the ("N") words they expel and you will learn to deflect negatives with your positive energy while maintaining your clarity. I will ask you again… "What do you want?" Remember I'm only asking because I always want you thinking about what you want and those thoughts will slowly become a way to Focus Forward. Everything you do should be focused and directed in a form of perpetual motion.

Perpetual Motion is a noun and it is defined as:

1) The hypothetical continuous operation of a mechanism without the introduction of energy from an external source known as perpetual motion of the first kind.

I want you to begin to see the internal energy that you produce from your Soul Step putting you in a constant state of positive. Your PDD will slowly become the "perpetual motion" to your success. The "N" word has to be kept at bay at all times and the motion you create and notice I said, "YOU" are the key to everything you want so think and choose wisely. As they say, "be careful what you wish for."

LIFE WORK JOURNAL ENTRY

I remember a conversation I had with my Dad one day. Okay, I didn't really remember it he reminded me about something I said when I was about 18 or 19 years old. We were talking about dream jobs and at the time I had already moved into my own apartment. I had a good job working at Ralph's Grocery Stores and I was also in college. I remember saying to him my dream job would allow me to travel all over the world and the pay for this job would be more money at that time than I had ever made. Let me tell you, I have flown on planes in the last twenty plus years more than I have personally driven a car. I have over eight hundred thousand miles on about five of the major airlines in the world. And guess what? I LOVE IT! As I remembered this statement I made to my father that day, I recall I truly believed in my heart I would be able to do this. Everything I have wanted or wanted to do thus far in my life, I have been focused enough, not lucky enough to do. You know what I say about luck. Luck does not exist in my world. That's my belief and I'm sticking to it.

END LIFE WORK JOURNAL ENTRY

"FOCUSED ENOUGH," again means you have done your homework in whatever it is you want to do and as opportunities are presented to you, you will be able to see, react, or receive them accordingly. Focused enough is what you get as you look in the mirror and see your goals being placed before you and as you see them, you know they are for you, and only you.

When you come to that realization, you won't allow fear to take it away from you. It's time to start believing in what you want as a reality. A major part of your reality is also understanding and having patience.

Patience is a noun and it is defined as:
1) The ability to endure waiting or delay without becoming annoyed or upset, or to persevere calmly when faced with difficulties.
2) The ability to tolerate being hurt, provoked, or annoyed without complaint or loss of temper.

Everyone has heard the phrase; "patience is a virtue" and to make any parts of FOCUS work for you, patience is extremely necessary. Remember, nothing happens overnight. Anything worth having is always worth working for, so you need to take your time in your assessment of what you want and please, be extremely careful what you ask for. There is a line in the Matrix where Morpheus is speaking to Neo, because Neo believes he is still bound by the laws that govern the Matrix. He says to Neo, "Free your mind." When he told Neo to free his mind, initially Neo did not have his soul step in check and a true belief in himself enough to complete his task. Neo was half way to completing his training and the "N" word crept in and caused a minor setback. Neo nearly failed at his task, but he learned never to give up on the mission and eventually he realized he had to learn patience. The point I'm trying to make is freeing your mind of all the superfluous negativity, so you can begin to see and accept your real world. You will always get what you give and you will definitely have what you say. The power in the tongue should never be under estimated and the conviction in your heart with those words will give you the strength necessary to find out, "WHAT YOU WANT!"

I believe everyone you meet and speak with, the conversations you have with these people, should have some meaning in your life. Even if it's just a "Hello, how are you?" You have no idea what you have just done for that person or yourself when you really mean what you say and take the time to really listen. I know for a fact several times in my life I've had some bad days and just a little smile from someone or a "Good Morning" on another occasion, was all I needed to get back on track. This one gesture brought me back to focused enough and did not allow the "N" word on that day to direct my emotions. As you continue to FOCUS on what you want another very important part of your FOCUS in this area is once you set goals start believing in them. When you set goals think about why you have and know there is a good reason for setting them.

Every self-improvement book I've ever read gives different ways for individuals to set goals. From: A lifework journal, creating picture boards, drawing up lists, writing each goal in order of priority, from the most attainable to the extremely way out there. The good thing about all of these methods is I believe they all work. Anything you can do that allows you to stay focused so you can succeed is truly a blessing. Setting goals is all about developing a routine for success. Every morning I get up and look in the mirror this has become a major part of my daily routine. I set a goal each and every day to be better today than I was yesterday and I do this during my daily affirmation. Many of us find "ROUTINE" to be boring, but I have to say routine is what makes a person great; from athletes to businessmen, teachers, actors, our firefighters and police officers, the routine these individuals create, allows them to get things done at a high level. None of their accomplishment could have been done without developing a routine, preparation and a belief in themselves. It takes fortitude and discipline to put in the work needed to achieve the goals you have set. I've always said, "If it were easy any and every one would be doing it!" It's certainly not easy to stand and stare at yourself in the mirror, but I have learned the necessary reasoning behind it. I ask myself, "What Do You Want"? When I asked that question I've been able to look within myself for the answer. No one can answer the question for you. Everyone's spirit and purpose are different, but I find it amazing how the Universe ties all of us together, helping us to help each other. There will be times when you and I will not meet our goals in the time we have set for ourselves but don't panic it's not in any way a failure. I believe everything I do is a learning experience teaching me lessons that I can only learn through doing. Every piece of knowledge you gain should be a part of the process of you. You are always the key for everything that happens in your environment and you will be the sum total of every experience you survive. Patience is learning to stop, look, and listen. Like I said before everything is right in front of you.

When you want something so badly you begin to see, taste, touch, hear and feel it's presence, then you know you're moving in the right direction. This is where thoughts of what you want begin to take on that three-dimensional appearance. They become very real and now you have them in your hand. In some cases, once people accomplish their goals by getting that dream job, business, house or person they worked so hard for, they can become complacent. They lose their FOCUS not remembering FOCUS doesn't stop when you reach a goal or fulfill a dream. This is when you really need to buckle down and continue to study, use that knowledge to continue the perpetual motion that got you to where you are today, SUCCESSFUL! You are the engine that drives everything you do and that's how your motion stays perpetual. As you become inspired and continue setting goal after goal and accomplishing them, keep in mind even though you have to do 95% of the work the last 5% comes from outside sources. We do nothing alone. Did you hear me? We do nothing alone and no man or woman is an island, and if they are we'll leave them out there. Yeah, I said it, leave them out there and let's see how far they get alone!

"SET AND BELIEVE," should be your mindset to FOCUS on the goals before you. Remember, as you set goals be sure you can meet them head on and they are attainable. How do they become attainable? To make your goals attainable you have to know the number one thing is always, always "DO YOUR HOMEWORK!" I'm going to say it as many times as it takes for you to get it. I'm trying to get you armed and keep you ready. During the period of my life I was dedicated to law enforcement and private security, there is a level of ready you have to maintain and after a while it becomes second nature. Your awareness of your surroundings can't be ignored and you must attempt to take in the whole picture whenever possible. To this day I always look to see the whole picture in everything I do. If you've learned something it's always yours, so use it. Wasted knowledge creates wasted effort and that is not how you live anymore.

The strength you find in the goals you set, will help you set the right goals and setting the right goals will enable you to reach and fulfill them by taking full advantage of every opportunity. Keep in mind the more you allow yourself to experience you'll keep flexing your FOCUS muscle and it will grow developing into what will become second nature. Along with setting goals and seeing what you want, there is a discipline that comes along with your FOCUS. Discipline works hand in hand, in the application of completing your goals and trusting the process. Having an idea or inspiration to do something is one thing, applying your FOCUS to move forward in goal setting, is another animal. Disciplined patience is a key factor in this area and as you begin to add more structure to your life, your disciplined patience will become as strong as you allow it to. Notice how I always put everything back on YOU. It's your FOCUS, it's your discipline, it's your patience and it's your Free Will. The bottom line in all this is, you have to believe! You make the conscious decision to do everything you do and the people and events you surround yourself with, set the positive you bring forth. It may seem like a lot of pressure, but trust me it's necessary. You have to learn to step up to the plate, look the pitcher square in the eye and with discipline, only swing at strikes over the plate. Don't' chase wild pitches by keeping your eye on the prize and maintaining your FOCUS. You have to put in the time every day to make a difference. I began writing this book as an outline for my own FOCUS and with discipline; I have been able to finish something else I started. Bigger, Better and always Stronger!

Because of the PDD that lives inside us we have an opportunity to follow our dreams and live our lives to the fullest. You're learning more about your Soul Step and what it means in your life and now you know the "N" word in any context is a very bad thing. You're learning to keep secrets for your own good and you have learned Focused Enough is where you always need to be. Most of all you know freeing your mind is not a drug altering experience, it's allowing your mind to do what it was created to do… GROW! Goal setting is a key component in developing your FOCUS. You should also know as you visualize, you would begin to see your life the way it should be seen. You have learned there are two sides to perpetual motion, the positive and the negative. You can move forward and look to live your life the way it should be or you can allow yourself to fall back and miss out on every opportunity placed before you. Remember what Larry Bird said about winners, with hard work this can be you. It's the only way you can win! And finally, you have learned that without discipline none of the above will ever work. Now that I have you thinking and looking to the positive, it's time you start, "Thinking Outside The Box."

5

Time To Think Outside The Box

To exist is to change, to change is to mature; to mature is to go on creating oneself endlessly...

Henri L. Bergson

Believe it or not...

The human body has some of the basic similarities of a box. The human body could be considered a large box with numerous small boxes inside. I know you're thinking... boy he is truly reaching with this one. I will admit I may be stretching this to a degree, but all I ask as I always do, is please be patient and bear with me. You've come this far so we can't stop now. Let's look at the definition of the word box.

Box, can be a noun or a verb and it is defined as;

1) **(NOUN)** A container, case, or receptacle, usually rectangular, of wood, metal, cardboard etc. and often with a lid or a removable cover.
2) **(VERB)** To strike with the hand or fist, especially on the ear.
3) **(VERB)** To fight against someone in a boxing match.

Boxes are used for many things, i.e. storage, transporting, separating protecting, and holding our most prized and valued possessions. They are also used for holding the food we eat. It's a stretch but please keep an open mind and work with me. Our bodies as a box? I bet you never looked at yourself quite like that have you? I want you to do what I asked you to do more than once in this book… Think! Remember everything you do, every day you live, begins with a thought. Also keep in mind every idea, from every person before you and every person hereafter will develop out of a thought, from thinking! Let's take a look at the word think…

Think is a verb and it is defined as…
1) To use the mind to consider ideas and make judgments.
2) To imagine or understand something or the possibility of something.

Each and every thought you have comes from a storage box located in your mind. Remember what I said about the use of words? Many of the words we use on a daily basis lose their power because we take them for granted, or we take away the power of these words, or we add negative power by the way we use them. We've forgotten the words we speak come from our thoughts, so as we think and speak, so shall we be and do. The strength and power words have in our lives are infinite in their design and will never return void, if you believe in them, positive or negative. I often think to myself and say things out loud to hear how they sound as these thoughts materialize. Many people and many bible scholars believe that God spoke the World, the Heavens and the Universe into existence from a single thought, that he then spoke out loud. These words being spoken and a belief that when he spoke these words they would come to pass. I'm not trying to turn this into bible study or religious class; I'm just giving you a little information from some of the research I have gathered. The power of your words, imagine that? Let's talk about thinking outside the box, or that mindset you're stuck in.

When I say it's time to think outside the box, what do I really mean by this? The main box I'm speaking of is your "MIND." It's time to open your mind to a new way of thinking, a new way of seeing, a new way of believing, but most of all a new way of living. Let's start with the composition of this box of yours. A box generally has four sides that are solid, a top and a bottom. The top and the bottom of the box are normally sealed shut to protect the contents inside. In every case the way boxes are packed and sealed is done by you, the owner. Now let's open your box so we can get you living outside of it.

The box, known as the human body is similar in fashion to a cardboard box. The human body also has four sides, a top and a bottom. The feet are the bottom and our head containing our brain or the mind is the top, or should I say this end up. Just like the box the human body is used for storage and transport. For the most part the body is one large box with several small boxes or compartments inside. The smaller boxes inside the body are not only there to keep things separated, but they also hold some of our most valued and prized possessions. Our heart along with our other vital organs, are our most prized possessions and each component of the human body, has its own box in a manner of speaking. I want you to do me a favor, close your eyes and see the box you are in. The box I refer to is the mindset that you live in every day. The mindset you live in is your "Soul Step" and that box is surrounded by influences on all sides, the top and bottom. The only way anything can get into your mind or your box, just like a real box, is if you put it in there. The only way anything can get into your "BOX" is if you put it in there!!! You control the box. You control the packing and unpacking of your box. Since you are the person who is responsible for everything you add or subtract from your box, it is your responsibility from time to time to purge your box. I bet you didn't think you had that much control over yourself? So now you're thinking to yourself… you mean to tell me that I'm the one who controls the box? Yes, that is what I mean to tell you. As I write this paragraph I can remember the day I began understanding how powerful my thoughts were, positive and negative. I can remember when I began to control what I said and how I said it. In my mid-thirties I made a conscious decision to treat everyone the way I wanted to be treated. (CLARITY IN OTHERS) I also remember during that time if I could do it, then what would happen if others jumped on the bandwagon and did the same? Oh, what a wonderful world, what a wonderful universe, this would be for us all. Treating everyone the way I wanted to be treated taught me respect.

Okay so I realized this might not happen on a worldwide scale anytime soon, but what about my immediate world? What about my environment? I asked myself, "What if I got everyone in my immediate circle to treat each other the way I wanted to be treated?" You talk about thinking outside the box. Having this happen could help to keep a majority of our lives always "Focus Forward" and positive. And think about everyone in your environment doing the same in their environment? Keeping an open mind is what you should always be thinking. I decided I would no longer let or allow one negative incident in the top of my morning, (NOTICE I SAID "MY MORNING") alter or dictate my emotional, physical, or spiritual attitude for the rest of that day. I am going to live my life the best way I can, positive and enjoying every second. Can you imagine the power a core group of people in your world would have, if they were all on one accord to do something positive? Now that's thinking outside the box. No one could stop you. Since we have a little more information about "THE BOX", let's take a closer look at how you packed yours. First things first, you have to accept the fact that you packed your box. If your box is filled with clutter, indecision, drama, or chaos, guess who put it there? Not me! I've packed and unpacked so many times it would make your head spin, but it is extremely necessary for you to stay focused and on top of things. That's enough about me; let's get back to you and the way you packed your box. During the packing and unpacking process, you're going to have to learn how to replace bad things or less desirable items in your box with good and positive items. But please remember there is no hurry to refill what you take out. Take your time everything in your life should be quality, not quantity! Less is sometimes better, I believe. The easiest way to do this is sit down and do a list of the pros and cons governing your life. This list will be a part of your "LIFEWORK JOURNAL" and in time this journal will become a way for you to look at your life with an objective eye and an open spirit. This journal is called your LIFEWORK JOURNAL, because we all need to take our lives a little more seriously when it comes to managing them and we have to understand that our lives are a constant "WORK" in progress every day. The things you write in the LJ need to be thought about openly and honestly. The LJ is a chance for you to be honest with yourself because it's for your eyes only. The LJ will become your strength and your FOCUS in tough times, because it could give you the outlet you need to keep you on track to a positive future. It could become the driving force in everything you do from the time it's created and it will also become one of your keys to success. I want you to write down how and why certain events affect you the way they do. Again, think hard and always be honest with yourself. The hardest part of self-evaluation is the honesty necessary to have with one's self. Opening up to look at yourself and possibly find or discover a kink in your armor is very difficult to do and live with, but you have to take that first step. The road less traveled, even though it's less traveled, is a road that now has to be traveled by "YOU." As you become more and more honest with yourself you will begin to learn and understand how to open your box allowing good things to happen and at the same time you will learn how to delete negative thoughts and feelings that continue to disrupt the flow of your FOCUS. This is not going to be easy by any stretch of your imagination, but anything worth having is always worth working for. Once your list is created and you begin being honest with yourself, the FOCUS you develop is what you will learn to use and that will enable you to start seeing with clarity in your life. Specifically, "Clarity in Purpose" will help you sort through the good and bad things in your box. And it could also give you a better understanding of why you do the things you do… or why you packed something, in your box in the first place. If items in your box are not helping you with your purpose, they must be removed. Sometimes seeing your life or the decisions you've made on paper, gives you an opportunity to see how you can make any necessary changes. Allowing things and situations to control your life and learning why these things happen will enable you to keep from making the same "WRONG" decisions, that have you in turmoil right now. Ending the negative cycle of circumstances surrounding our lives can change our mindset thereby creating positive circumstances, leading to a positive existence. I want you to understand making this list is crucial to your positive future. These two list; the pros and cons of your life will become the grocery list that you will learn to shop from, to unpack and repack your box. Using clarity in everything you do creates such a positive environment the "N" word can even be used in a positive light. It's kind of like the anti-hero in a story… hiding in the shadows waiting for the right moment to strike. Even though he or she is the anti-hero they can still save the day.

Thinking outside the box, through your mind and spirit, can be an extremely tough thing to do. We believe staying in our box tucked away in our environment is what will keep us safe. For many of us we believe our lives can't get any better, or we don't deserve better than what we have, or who we've become. This couldn't be further from the truth. You could be right on the cusp of creating something amazing and because the thoughts you're having don't line-up with your "REGULAR" thinking, you let it go sending it back into the Universe for another to discover. Every thought, idea, brain cramp, or fraction, of a fraction of that fraction, of anything you think was given to "YOU" to use. You have to be prepared to change, mature and learn to re-create yourself in order to have an opportunity for success.

Understanding how people and situations control your life, and learning why we allow this to happen. This could enable us to control them so they don't happen again, or continue to control us, thereby ending the negative cycle in our lives and changing the negative circumstances plaguing our existence. Since you've begun making your list I want you to understand that this step is extremely important. These two lists, the pros and cons of your life will become the grocery list you can learn to shop from. I believe we have all been shopping at some point in our lives, on some level. Whether it's shopping for food, or clothing, a car, whatever the shopping we've all done our fair share. Before making a major purchase most of us create a list of the item(s) we wish to buy, by making comparisons with similar products or brands. We spend a lot of time making lists for the market, cutting out coupons from newspapers or magazines. We look for the best deal that will make our lives easier and save us as much money and time as possible. We research the internet anytime we decide to make a major purchase of a car, or even household appliances. Again, looking for the best price and most of all the highest quality in the products we want to purchase. We will dedicate hours upon hours trying to find and then negotiate a deal for ourselves, but when it comes to looking in the mirror at ourselves, when it comes to self-evaluation we don't apply the same amount of time or energy. You have to realize you are worth more than anything you could purchase in a store or order over the Internet. Taking the time to work on "YOU" has to become your priority.

We don't apply the same amount of energy for ourselves, because at times we don't care about number one. You are number one and in order for you to "HELP" others you have to be willing and able to help yourself. We always look for those great deals on the material things in life because having nice things makes people, (looking in from the outside) like you. We all want to be liked on some level… don't we? I have found if people like the things you have, in most cases they don't really know you, so how do you know if they really even like you? How many times have you seen a celebrity on top of the world, their entourage is thirty-people deep and they are riding the wave of success? Now that's a box in need of being purged. I've seen this way too many times. Then a mistake here and there and we see their public fall from grace. Now when you see this person minus all the nice flashy stuff, he or she is now, all alone. One of the most important things you will discover over time is, everything having to do with your success starts with you "LOVING" yourself. When you are all alone at night and you have that 5 minutes before you go to sleep, and take a look back at your day... are you happy with everything and everyone in your box? Everyday major corporations all over the world spend billions on what they call, "BRAND RECOGNITION". A brand in many cases is a product and through advertising these companies have found ways to make their "BRAND" recognizable for us the consumers. In the last ten to fifteen years' individuals have become the brand. I have a friend, Leslie Short of, K.I.M. Media and her motto is "You are the brand!" If you believe this analogy do you want to be a superior brand like Mac or Netflix, or would you like to be some fly by night-company that never gets established? Even though these major corporations and their "BRANDS" are recognized worldwide, they all started with a thought, in most cases from a single individual, to become who and what they are today.

This is the reason your pros and cons list have to be important! It's going to make you begin to think! Oh boy, there's that "THINK" word again. As you study your two lists and begin to think about your life, I want you to look at adding and subtracting items from each list when appropriate, just as you do when you go shopping. Look at it as if you're shopping for a new way to live your life. It's also a new way to start looking at the lives of everyone you come into contact with. As you evaluate each list, learn to read the list as ingredients in the foods you buy and if you decide one day you don't like a particular ingredient anymore, remove it from your list. That's how you begin a lifestyle change. FOCUS will become a key asset in everything you do. As soon as you start deleting the negatives from your con list, the pros will begin to give you more clarity in your vision, and purpose.

Clarity will come into play as you start thinking outside the box is the norm. Negative ("N") words, or negative thought processes that once controlled your thinking will not make sense to you anymore. As they say, "Out with the old and in with the new." The positive thoughts and dreams you've always had will have the opportunity to evolve or develop and create a new way of living. The re-evaluation of your life is necessary in the re-construction of your mind's eye and your Soul Step. Keep in mind as we learn more about ourselves through an honest evaluation, then and only then will we see growth in ourselves, helping us to live better lives, by creating a stronger Soul Step. Your Soul Step is developing inside you every day. As your attitude begins changing this will lead you to a clearer path for success. I hope you heard that! As you continue living you will discover, you get out of life, what you put in. Developing a strong enough mind set to think outside the box is a process that cannot be rushed, but the earlier you learn and begin working on it, the sooner you'll see opportunities as they present themselves. I know I keep harping on being aware of opportunities and recognizing they are meant for you, but this is one of the driving forces behind the Unlikely Destiny, series of books. Self-awareness breed's universal awareness and universal awareness gives meaning and balance to your purpose. When your purpose is confirmed or understood, directed steps will always follow.

Thinking outside the box means, we have to stop and look at the world we live in and the people we surround ourselves with, and this will allow us to break the mold of negativity. I've said it before but it's worth saying again, "We have lived in the negative for so long we believe this is our new normal. This normal will continue to destroy us, if we don't learn to see and think outside the box." Your life is and should be better than that and the people you share your life with, they deserve your best, and you deserve better from them. Looking at the box you live in, you will get out of it, what you put into it. Did I say that again? If it's filled with clutter you're the one who filled it. Learn to take a deep breath and look to let things happen in their time, but continue to always look and live your life in the positive.

Take a minute or two, to really look at yourself. If your feelings on a daily basis are "FOUL" and the tongue you speak with is "NEGATIVE," then guess what? That's what you will get! We get what we give in everything we do and these are the things we fill our box with. If you don't believe in "YOU," it's going to be hard for others to do so. It may sound simple and believe me in some cases it is, but for some because they have lived the "N" word for so long, the transition can be extremely difficult, but you can change. Thinking outside the box could be as simple as changing your sox, or putting on a pair of pants. If you look at your "LJ" and you see what you have been doing is not in any way making your life better, then just pause or stop, drop and roll. Stop putting up with people and situations that don't generate anything positive in your life! Drop bad attitudes and anyone who puts you in situations of stress or ridiculous conflict! Roll yourself away from every individual or circumstance that does not fit in line with the idea you have for your life! Words have the positive and negative power we give them. Keep that in mind when you're drafting your next text message or that email to a loved one or a co-worker. Just because they are not standing in front of you doesn't mean they don't hurt. Because of technology it has made it easy for us not to see the human factor in our lives anymore. Remember how you want to feel in your relationships and most of all, how you want to be treated. You have to transfer those same feelings to everyone you meet and if you learn to do this you will understand: you get what you give.

Here comes one of those free will statements… Your life! Your control! When you wake up every day your goal should be to always think outside the box, because this is where you need to live. You can't play it safe forever so open your eyes and let your mind run free. Fear stopped me from writing this book several years ago. I woke up one day several months before I started writing this book and said to myself, it's time to write "UNLIKELY DESTINY." As I looked at and evaluated my list, I took UNLIKELY DESTINY off my cons list and allowed myself to see my life, the way things should be. The writer that I am was always there; I just chose not to accept it, because fear still controlled parts of my life. That's how many of us are, fear controls parts or aspects of our lives, not allowing us to see and use the "Whole World." One day your fear has to become your fuel. The fear of thinking outside the box has to become that needed stepping stone, moving you to the next level of enlightenment. "Fear and the box," sounds like a children's book written by Stephen King. Fear is one of our biggest adversaries. The "F" word has stopped or slowed the focus forward thinking of many an idea and it has also torn apart many lives and countless friendships. I have a reminder quotes for you… "If you don't see the vision, don't you stop the dream!" I created this quote and it runs deep in my spirit for those who don't understand your journey, or care to understand your journey. It's a way for me to maintain my FOCUS, keeping my eye on what I consider my prize. Just remember everyone has a purpose and even though you may not understand his or her PDD to do something, just try and be supportive, PERIOD!

LIFEWORK JOURNAL ENTRY

I had so many dreams I lost count, but I never gave up dreaming. There were several people living in my neighborhood and several teachers who didn't know it at the time, but they were what I would call "DREAM CRUSHERS." If you spoke about things you wanted to do other than playing some sort of sport, they either told you, you couldn't do something or they didn't give you any type of encouragement to fulfill those dreams. Not every teacher, but there were a few and the thoughts that resonate the loudest was their lack of encouragement, or their overall ignorance. Doing anything outside the norm of what they thought my environment may be, was totally out of the question. Today I am extremely happy I was always an individual who chose not to listen to the "DREAM CRUSHERS." Because I learned to "PLAY" early in life, this became the Focus Forward ideal I'm living today.

END LIFEWORK JOURNAL ENTRY

There were periods when I was younger that I got discouraged, but I never stopped writing. I took creative writing classes when I could and every time I had a writing assignment in English class I would literally salivate at the thought of writing a fictitious story. I thank God I never gave up on the dream of becoming a writer. A major component of thinking outside the box is having dreams, which you need to form a vision, to give your dreams tangibility. Your dreams will develop clarity because you are learning to evaluate yourself and your surroundings, thus allowing you to make strong and sound decisions. What do you think about your box now? Wrap that sucker up and put a bow on it! "YOU" are the only person stopping "YOU" from living your dreams and reaching your goals. People or obstacles may get in your way, but that's to be expected. Your obstacles have to become your stepping stones. That has to be your mindset going in to keep your PDD moving in the right direction. You will begin to welcome obstacles because we love and need the challenge. As your awareness increases and the box you control becomes balanced to the pro side of your life, your FOCUS will become so much more valuable to you. Thinking Outside the Box (T.O.T.B.) is extremely necessary to move forward and find the success you are looking for. Positive visions of success are also extremely important as you learn to visualize. In your visualization you can clearly see, where you are going and learn to do, What Is Necessary, to get there (WIN). What is necessary for your success? This is something you'll have to determine, but I can guarantee you this, none of this gets done without hard work and a belief in yourself! Something that has helped me in writing and completing this book is seeing it completed! The main piece to my visualization puzzle is going to several bookstores, standing in the section that relates to me and I see my book "UNLIKELY DESTINY VOLUME ONE," on the shelf. People are walking by picking it up and looking at it. They open it, read my introduction or they look at the back cover and read my bio. Then they buy it. Oh, what a rush!!! It is extremely necessary that as you visualize, you believe you have set and completed every aspect of your dreams. T.O.T.B.

Think about the feelings you get when you set, meet and or accomplish your goals. This is the same feeling that will kick your Soul Step to new levels. That level is developing an awareness of everything before you and everything to come. The box you are creating is setting a new dynamic in thinking, seeking, believing, self-confidence and most of all you will ascend to a new level of Enlightenment. T.O.T.B. is what has moved me to the mindset I have today, I have always had an entrepreneur's heart and every day you have to believe in what you are doing, more than anyone else. Having that mind set not only keeps you thinking two steps ahead of everyone, but it also forces you to look at every side, of everything you do. It's kind of like looking at every side, top and bottom of a box. The simplicity of T.O.T.B. as you create your lists, on both the pros and cons, of some things, you almost need to do the opposite of what you are presently doing. It may sound too easy to be true, but just think about it for a minute. Do the opposite… are you thinking? If you are not, "THINKING" I just proved my point. If there have been times you decided to go left, then maybe next time you go right or vice versa. If you continue to think outside the box, this will always leave you open to try new things and when you open yourself up to anything new, help will always present itself.

Remember "YOU" are the key to every bit of your success and failures. The inner strength you develop, as you begin to build your character will pay off for you in ways you never imagined. Or have you? I told you before the sky's the limit. Well I'm going to have to change that because now that you're aware you help to give our Universe balance, and the Universe has no boundaries, why should you? You have to be thinking about that one. The box that makes you who you are is going to be a blessing to you and those you meet. Everything you do, every place you go and every one you come in contact with, has purpose and reason in your life. As you begin to T.O.T.B. you have to see your life this way. So, you're thinking, analyze every part of my life, every part of my day? Yes, this is what you must do. The best way for you to see a better life is to look for a better life. T.O.T.B. is just the beginning, because acting on those thoughts as we have discussed before must become a mandatory function. As your FOCUS develops you will learn to see through and filter out all the clutter in front of you. Keep in mind, I don't want you to drive yourself crazy with every detail of every day, but you do need to understand that they exist and the little things always matter. You haven't done it up to this point and look at where you are? The box can be a good place to live your life from as long as you remember it is ever changing, and as it changes you must adapt to those changes. This is the only way to keep your box somewhat clutter free.

Growing up, as far back as I can remember I've been a little different. Possibly, because of the thoughts and dreams I've had and the choices I've made. Sometimes I felt a little weird or maybe just a little bit, like I didn't fit in, where I was at the time. I still feel that way at times! I explained in an earlier chapter growing up in Watts and Compton California was at times extremely difficult. When a large group of your peers go left and you and a select few go right, that could make you want to crawl into a box. The peer pressure I experienced back then, I can still feel as I write this paragraph. There is a true-life pressure you feel when a friend pushes you to do something and you have to push back. As a child the thought of losing what you believe is a friend, could be devastating. Was this person a true friend? When I look at my idea of a friend, maybe not! It may sound a little dramatic, but sometimes I had to walk alone. As kids everything negative was devastating. We dream big and we fall hard, but we always get back up! I always had the fear my father would find out I did something stupid, and like I said before, he didn't play! I will continue to say to you, "Things happen in your life the way they are supposed to." I didn't realize it at as a child, but I thought outside what was my preverbal box by not becoming my environment. I didn't become a criminal, nor did I join a gang. I didn't sell or do drugs, but most importantly I never let myself down by doing anything I didn't want to do! Often time's people think because you didn't get into a lot of trouble, you don't know what trouble is. Just because I didn't join the crips, doesn't mean I don't know what a gang is. I don't have to kill someone to know they are dead! My point is I've learned to look at negative situations from a distance and I feel it's one of the best ways to learn, but believe me I have seen and experienced my share of devastating situations. I believe the life you are given should be lived to the fullest and you should never short change your life experiences out of fear. Fear is the greatest enemy inside and outside of your box. It will keep you caged like an animal in the zoo. Fear will take a great idea you have and crush it like a bug hitting your windshield on the highway going nowhere. Fear is going to constantly find a way to get into your box and that's why you're going to have to purge your box on a regular basis. T.O.T.B. should become a destination in the success of restructuring your life. As you T.O.T.B. FOCUS will allow you to live and understand your Unconscious Consciousness as you move into a constant perpetual motion.

If you look at the life you're living, and you can honestly see room for improvement then you're going to have to take a step at making a change. As you look at the L.J. you've created, you may have to do something drastic! What do you have to lose except a bad attitude and maybe a few negative people? Yes, you may have to push the delete button on some of the relationships that have kept the "N" word (NEGATIVE) and the "F" word (FEAR) ever present in your life. There is an old saying and it goes like this ***"MISERY LOVES COMPANY."*** Think about it and if you don't remember anything I've said, remember this… It speaks for itself: ***"MISERY LOVES COMPANY."*** Think about how many people you've met who never do anything positive, or never have anything, not one positive thing to say… you know who and what I'm talking about.

Take a really hard look at how they are living their lives. One of the best things about their situation is you don't have to live it with them. You see as we meet people and develop relationships we are not always focused and often times we lose our way. We start living our lives according to the relationships we develop, or allow ourselves to put up with. We can also get so caught up in the negative hype of others and forget about our goals, dreams, and aspirations. Something I've learned as a listener is, no matter how many people I have listened to, or helped in their lives, I still have to live my own. There will be times when you will have to set guidelines and boundaries, for your friends and especially family. Yes, I said family! They are sometimes the worst because they are family and don't expect you to mind if they impose on your life. Okay you can stop laughing. I'm not telling you to cut all those people off at the knee, but what I am saying is watching what you say around them, will help to keep the pressure off of you, as you work toward completing your mission. I like to look at projects as missions; because missions are often covert and you need to maintain your status as a covert operative. As you learn to think outside the box, keep in mind you are on a new path to freedom. Albeit new, it's truly your new path. Most people won't understand the balance you've created through self-evaluation and the development of your Soul Step, but that's okay. It's okay they don't understand and I don't want you to lose your FOCUS trying to convince them, so keep it to yourself. As your development continues, they can't help but see your PDD and determination begin to shine thorough. We all live in a place that protects us…" The Box." Now here I am asking you to give up that protection and step outside your comfort zone. I'm asking you to take a chance and do something different. Do something that is going to give you a different and, in most cases, a better outcome than you've had before. It's a lot to ask you to give up the life you are currently living and try something different, but if your current situation is filled with negativity and fear, among other things, what do you have to lose? You need to move Focus Forward in so many areas of your life, but the if "N" and the "F" continue to dominate you like, Shaquille O'Neal guarding the basket, you'll have to find another way to score. (NEXT OPTION) Please do me a favor, take two steps back and give your life an honest look. Without honesty T.O.T.B. will never work and because it doesn't, you won't be able to develop the mental strength necessary, to begin living your life to the fullest.

I constantly re-evaluate my life; looking at who I am and what I'm doing several times a year. Trust me it's necessary to help you maintain control over the negative forces. When I find myself losing FOCUS, losing patience or falling short of my goals, I reset and give myself a swift kick in the ass, then I re-boot my hard drive, or my Soul Step to re-establish my purpose. I re-focus on my goals and just keep it moving! T.O.T.B is the world you want to live in, so pack your bags and let's go there. Everyone who lives in this world has learned to be a free thinker. They've learned they will make mistakes and the world will not end. I said it before you're going to make a mistake here and there, but it's how quickly you recover after the mistake that will separate you from everyone else. Delete any mistakes, so they don't get into your spirit or start developing as clutter or negativity.

I love sports, especially basketball, football, mixed martial arts (MMA), tennis, boxing and golf. I love sports with such a passion my friends laugh at me when I pace the floor and yell at the television if my team, or a particular player is not playing up to their potential. I am fascinated when I see an athlete break out of his or her shell for the first time and develop the FOCUS necessary to become a great player. I am also fascinated when I see that same player, have the worst game of his or her life, and in less than 24 hours, they refocus and completely dominate their opponent again. How does that happen? It has to be FOCUS! These extraordinary people are just that, people! I've said it before, they are human and the only thing making them special is they believe. They believe in themselves and they have thought outside the box so many times, they are not afraid of being out there, and they also do their homework! It has become the norm in their lives and that's the way they live, or as they say, "THAT'S HOW WE ROLL."

They believe whatever it is they are doing; they are the best! Even the athlete, who may not be a "Superstar" believes in himself and has faith that they are supposed to be where they are. A role player on any team is just as important as the star player because they have to believe just as much as the superstar, that they are able to do their job to the best of their abilities. All the moving parts working together as one unit to complete their goals. This falls right in line with what I have been saying about helping each other. Sometimes the best way to see the "help" factor at its best is to look at the team concept. The starting five of a basketball team, or the eleven starters of a football team, all have a role to play on offense and defense. Out of every starter there are some amazing athletes, and even though the team has a "Superstar" they must work as a team to have a chance at winning. Remember Michael Jordan, as great as he was with a basketball, didn't win his first NBA Championship until after his 7th season in the NBA. Each member of their particular team knows the strengths and weakness of the player next to him or her. They don't get angry or upset with the player to their left or right because they are honest in their assessment of themselves. They learn to give and take when necessary or in simple terms they learn to help. "A rising tide lifts all boats." There has to be a give and take in your self-evaluation, and you have to be willing to do both.

From Opportunity Comes Unlimited Success, is not just a phrase that begins or completes a sentence! It can and is truly a way of life for me and for those who won't allow themselves to lose sight of their dreams of success, prosperity, and happiness. As they say "Always keep your eye on the prize," but you have to decide what that prize is. In this process of learning to think outside the box we have to find out everything we can about where we want to go and the information necessary to get us there. Self-evaluation coupled with your P.D.D. topped off with a lot of hard work, will always equal growth in whatever you're doing and in every area of your life. The box you have developed over the years has been forged in most cases out of fear. When you don't understand how fear controls your life, you could spend your entire existence living that way. Since you are learning what has controlled the outcome of most of the events in your life, to this point, it's time to make a change. Change can be hard to accept, but as you learn to do it, the box you live in, will no longer control you. You will begin learning to control every aspect of your life. See the door, open the door and step through to the other side. It sounds easy right? It can and will be when you learn to adjust the dial on your attitude to positive. We walk through doors every day without any direction, fear, or reservation and we survive. We do this every day several times a day without thinking about the consequences. We need to learn to maintain the same strength of mind that we have in routine situation and apply that same sense of calm and patience to complex situations. Being and living positive is not as hard as we make it as long as you remember that it works both ways.

Anyone can be positive when things are going well, but what do you do when it seems like the walls are caving in? You adjust your attitude like I said, by controlling what you say and continue to believe in yourself and don't look at the circumstances plaguing your life at present, but learn to have faith in your abilities. As you continue to do this people around you, (NOT THAT YOU ARE TRYING TO IMPRESS THEM) will begin to notice the change. Your attitude will create a chain reaction creating a positive explosion that will be felt throughout the known Universe. Your positive attitude will begin to attract positive people and positive situations that will seem to come to you out of nowhere, or is it by design? Believe it or not, it is by design. Your design when you opened a positive gate in our Universe, releasing the power of your strength to accomplish goals you have set.

Remember your attitude is like a positive, focused, ball of energy and what you do with that energy will affect our planet, your environment and the Universe. T.O.T.B. your attitude and your energy will not only affect your day, but the day of everyone you come in contact with. Positive or negative your Soul Step should always be Focus Forward and FOCUS Positive. Everyone around you will receive the energy you expel, even when you don't think your mood or behavior can affect your family, friends, co-workers or your employees, it does. Even your voice over the phone can change the temperament of the person on the other end, causing them to give back the same positive or negative energy! Your FOCUS should be a constant reminder for you to treat those around you, always the way you want to be treated. Your box is ever changing and the box you started with has been opened, emptied out and repacked with, FOCUS as your new guide.

This day can be the first days of the rest of your life. Yes, it's cliché, but it is so true because the world and the way you look at it will no longer be the same. I keep telling you to think about the things I have written, but I'd also like for you to think about this… you can make the changes necessary, by thinking outside your old box and using the new knowledge you've acquired. As you start seeing the world around you in a new light, that light will begin to envelop you and show you things you've never seen before. If there is an opportunity being placed before you… what are you going to do? I will answer that for you…TAKE IT! Knowing things happen in your life the way they are supposed to, is amazing knowledge and you will not be denied ever again.

A part of learning to think outside the box is developing a new attitude about yourself and your belief system. What do you believe? Do you believe you can do the things you think you can? I do! How much of what you know do you believe? If knowledge is one of the true keys to success, and if doors can be opened with the keys you've acquired in your life, then it's time to start opening doors. No one is going to open them and no one is going to hand you the success you think you deserve. Notice I said, "THINK" you deserve? You have to know you deserve any and everything you are willing to work for. And once you know this, the people around you will also know. The Soul Step you are learning to live your life by will reflect back to everyone you come in contact with. Good habits and a positive attitude are extremely contagious! Living and understanding you have the ability to control certain aspects of your life, is the clarity I live every day. I truly understand the power I've gained, knowing I can control the power over my thoughts and dreams. My "FOCUS", is one of the biggest blessings I could ever have and I know that, T.O.T.B. is how I begin and end each day. That is up to me! The attitude I leave the house with, is up to me! I know the clarity I live my life by, is on track allowing my success to be fulfilled. Beginning the process of thinking outside the box is just that: "A PROCESS." You have to allow yourself to follow through the process by, learning to trust the process. If you're reading this right now I hope you are seeing something you didn't before. Maybe a new way of seeing your environment, with a positive twist. Looking at your family, friends, co-workers and employees, as human before anything else. We will always be more than most people see in us at first glance. As you look at the two lists you have prepared, you will need to evaluate what it is you have written, with an open mind, heart, and an honest eye, so change is able to take place. To quote Albert Einstein "Intellectual growth should commence at birth and cease only at death." I look at the life I live and I am reminded it is an everyday process to look within to find the difference I chose to make in my life. Again, I'm happy in the knowledge I have a real say in my own life and its direction.

If you're used to flying solo or doing things on your own and in all these years you haven't made any headway, then maybe you need a little help. Don't be afraid to ask for the help you might need. This is thinking outside the box. Fear in many cases is what will keep you from asking for help. I've been there I know a little bit about that. Sometimes just asking for that little bit of help could make the difference in failure and success. Even athletes who play individual sports like golf, or tennis, cycling, or even the big, bad MMA fighter, all need coaches, sparring partners, etc. They all need a team! In other words, they need "HELP" to get from point A to point B, and so will you in order to be successful. We like success!!! If you allow yourself to always be in a guarded state, that will get you nowhere fast. Living your life guarded is like a closed fist… NOTHING IN! NOTHING OUT! They're really only good for one thing: punching and you can't punch everything all the time. Maybe you're one of those people that refuses to listen to anyone or advice? Well maybe you need to start listening and trust me on that one because I'm a listener. Looking back over my life, I can see parts and pieces of FOCUS I did not recognize back then, but I know how and why certain things happened and now, I understand their purpose or the process by which they've happened now. (CLARITY IN MEMORY)

This is going to sound crazy, but I know the life I'm living is mine and I'm happy it is. The experiences I've lived through helped me in a strange way and allowed me to recognize and understand FOCUS. With every ounce of my spirit I believe my FOCUS strengthens my soul and lifts my spirit to help me see the true lights in our Universe. Every second in my life I know, I wouldn't trade any of my experiences good or bad, for anything in the world. I've had to travel every road; dealt with every situation with the limited knowledge I had at the time, to gain the knowledge and insight I have today. I believe through these experiences we gain the knowledge and wisdom that is needed to spark the beginning of understanding our FOCUS. Talk about an epiphany! How many times have you heard someone say? "If I only knew then what I know now." I have to say I've heard this said at least a million times. Or here's a better one, how about "Hindsight is 20/20." (CLARITY IN MEMORY) A better way to start looking at yourself in these situations is to know that you have grown. Grown as a person, as a father, a mother, a sister or a brother or even a friend. Knowing a major part of growth comes from life experience, but a better part of that growth comes from learning through the life experiences of others. (CLARITY IN OTHERS) Okay since I said it, it's time for you to learn from one of my experiences. As I've gotten older I have come to understand or should I say I've grown to a point of Enlightenment in the knowledge that each and every experience is placed before us so we can grow. The good and especially the bad! I believe each experience has your name on it. Think about that for a minute... If you only had good things happening to you what would you learn? How would you grow? Bottom line you wouldn't! As a child in school if you made it to the sixth grade and for the next ten years you didn't move from that grade how would you ever continue to grow other than physically? Character is built and lives are changed through adversity and with these challenges, if you pay close attention you'll learn to think outside the box.

LIFEWORK JOURNAL ENTRY

I look at the move I made from Los Angeles to New York and at the time I didn't know the true reason why that move across country was necessary. My FOCUS at the time was only a partial developing thought. It had not yet grown to a vision of Enlightenment. Here's what I learned. Understanding that things happen in your life the way they are supposed to, I have to believe in order to move forward with Unlikely Destiny, I had to make the trek across country, to fulfill this portion of my life. The main thing I learned from being and living in New York City is patience. Patience taught me to look at people in a way that allows me to step outside the box at all times and not base my first impression of anyone on our first encounter. Everyone and I mean everyone deserves a second, third and fourth chance, just like the one I'm living today. That simple step also taught me to be physically, mentally, spiritually and emotionally stronger. It prepared me to deal with the world, by being able to slow everything down, so I didn't lose "ME." New Yorkers move at two speeds: fast and faster, so being able to T.O.T.B. allows me the opportunity to adapt to each and every situation with minimal stress. The patience I have learned to stand on has helped me to become a better listener and most of all a better writer. This has also allowed the box I live outside of, to always grow to the positive. The main benefit in this learning process is to separate myself from each situation I'm involved in, so I can look and see the positive in that situation and the people that are involved.

END LIFEWORK JOURNAL ENTRY

Being able to maintain my FOCUS at the highest level allows me to constantly filter the non-sense out of my life. That constant filter helps to keep your stress level down and it also helps to keep your box open to free thinking. If you're open to free thinking without limits or boundaries, just think how far you can go in this Universe of ours. How far you decide to go is all up to you. Free will doesn't limit us; we limit ourselves by not reaching for our goals, or truly exercising our "FREE WILL!" Think about this, free will is yours and the best thing about it; no one can ever take it from you! You will only be limited because you allow it. We all have dreams that have been with us since we can remember. Sometimes we lose ourselves, or sight of our dreams, because we let bad nonsense fill up our box, killing our dreams and causing our lives to sometimes spin out of control. This is another "DREAM CRUSHER." My goal is to make you truly think about your life outside the box. To take a look at some of the things that have happened to you, to help you understand, the reason they happened and hopefully help you not make them again. I also want you to start looking at how you've reacted to the things that have happened to you. Sometimes the reaction you have to your environment is what has kept you from moving forward. I also looked at the reservations I had at the time of my move across country. Leaving my son, my family, and friends was extremely hard, but I believe it was the best thing for me at that time. Moving could be the best thing for you, but you have to be open and willing to do it.

You don't have to stop loving those close to you, just because you move to another city, or state. In the world we live in today, with the technology that we hold in the palm of our hands, or at the touch of a computer, we can always stay in touch. Don't allow a move to another city be it near or far, to affect the outcome of your future. Sometimes a move could be the beginning, to spark the flame, fueling the fire for you to succeed. Thinking outside the box! You could also look at it as leaving a negative environment, but you need to assess that for yourself. Thinking outside the box! In order to move Focus Forward, this may sound silly, but you have to look forward and step in that direction. If you think about this country's history, many people from all parts of the world have come to the United States of America to find their success, and here you are. Success has always been inside you... you just have to learn to let it out. Now that we've opened your box and listed the pros and cons (Lifework Journal). You've taken a look at the concept of your body being the most complex box you own. You should be getting a better understanding of yourself living outside of your box, as a reality. Your next reality is learning that you must Be Open To Any And Everything (BOTAAE). Free your mind...

6

Being Open To Any And Everything "BOTAAE"

Observe constantly that all things take place by change, and accustom thyself to consider that the nature of the Universe loves nothing so much as to change the things which are, and to make new things like them...

Marcus Aurelius

Welcome to Chapter 6. I say welcome and I thank you for reading up to this point and I hope you have received as much gratification reading my words, as I have writing them thus far. In the first five chapters I've given you some insight into my life as the writer of this book, but I've also asked a lot of you as the reader. In my Introduction, I opened up my life and near-death experience, revealing how thankful I am for my second chance at life. With that second chance, I know I have a lot more work to do. In Chapter One, I asked you to think about your destiny. I told you what "DESTINY" means to me and how I have been able to shift my life in a positive direction through understanding, From Opportunity Comes Unlimited Success, allowing me the ability to write, "Unlikely Destiny." In Chapter Two, I asked you to take a look into yourself by looking in a mirror, in order to help you see with clarity to increase your Soul Step. In Chapter Three I asked the age-old question "Why Are You Here?" and after you took a deep look into your soul, I hope you came to a better understanding of your purpose and how "PURPOSE" should direct your life and your steps, giving balance to our Universe. In Chapter Four, I asked you to look at and think about why you are here? I hope that gave you a clearer FOCUS to understand what you want, thereby increasing your focused direction. Then I asked you to use all the insight I hope you've acquired in the first four chapters and in Chapter Five, I asked you to think outside the proverbial box by clearing out all the negative clutter. T.O.T.B. allows you to believe beyond your circumstances to live the life you deserve. Now in Chapter 6, a whole new Universe is at your doorstep waiting for you to open the door and step up to recognize you can create a better environment. It's okay to take that first step, because you should finally be working outside the box. Let's see how far we can go, or how deep this rabbit hole takes us. I know you are in the right place with your Soul Step and because you are, this will give you the opportunity of, "Being Open To Any And Everything," (BOTAAE).

While the box you call home is still open and it has been newly decorated in attitude, mindset, belief and opinion, your new reality should be, it's okay to believe in yourself. Believing in "YOU" has to become your new social behavior. I know I told you, so many people, have lived doom and gloom for so long; they begin to believe that's how their lives are supposed to play out. How can you live your life to the fullest when "YOU" won't allow yourself to? How can you begin to understand the life you're living, when the truth does not ring free in your life? Free is one of those words we use far too often that I believe has lost the truth, in its meaning to us. Let's take a look at the word "free"

Free is an adjective and it is defined as…
1) Not controlled, restricted, or regulated by any external thing.
2) Not or no longer physically bound or restrained.
3) Not subject to censorship or control by a ruler, government or other authority and enjoying civil liberties.

The point I'm trying to make with all of the "FREE" talk is the first step to freedom, is inside you. I can't stress enough the importance your Soul Step plays in your freedom. You can be as free as you allow yourself to be. I have spoken with and read studies about inmates who have been incarcerated for more than twenty plus years and they've all said, learning to be free starts in your spirit, mind and eventually it makes its way to your body. They learned to free their minds from incarceration by creating their own reality, not allowing the mind to adjust to a restricted environment. Learning to think outside the box is the first step in learning to open up and allowing your imagination to function freely. Observe constantly that all things take place by change and because everything changes, that is truly one of the constants we can always look forward to. With change you must be willing to do the same, "CHANGE." If you don't look to change even in the slightest, you will never grow or evolve on any level of your life. Without growth you will never be able to think outside the box you're living in. This will cause you to continue to be trapped never allowing you the freedom to live a better life. Being open to any and everything is the next step in shedding the bonds of negativity that are holding you down. The cycle of negativity has to stop somewhere. It's all up to you… BOTAAE. As I began writing this book I kept the idea of the book to myself only telling a select few. I know, I know, I told you to keep the things you are doing or working on to yourself. I know I said this, but here are a couple of exceptions to this rule.

1) You can only discuss information such as this with the people who truly understand you and are supportive in your life.
2) You have learned, to use people who live the world of negativity to your advantage. Their negativity will motivate you to focus forward and never give up.

I told a select few I was writing a book that I hoped would motivate people to want to do something positive with their lives, but most importantly I want people to think! My motivation grew at the thought of writing my book and I begin to believe in my purpose as a writer. I began to see everything around me in a different light and that light also revealed to me, who really had my back, according to their comments about me writing a book. The three people I chose to tell I was going to write a book, as I made my way through Chapter Two "Look In The Mirror," I realized something. This idea began as a Nano bite of space in my spirit and continued to grow, into what is my Soul Step today. The confidence that grew in me every day, is as tangible as the nose on my face. The first three people I told, is because they are the most motivated, positive and extremely focused people, in my life and I knew they would get the concept and have my back without question. They backed me with strength and encouragement and their support means the world to me. But, I still had to write the book myself. The other small group of people I decided to tell about the book didn't live their lives on the positive side of the Universe. They live their lives in "Negative City." They also responded the way I thought they would. From questioning my ability to write a book, to sending every negative dart or arrow with a joke, they could my way. When they asked, "How's the book coming?" or "Are you finished writing that book yet?" Deep down in my spirit I know they wanted me to say, I had given up and I would not be finishing my book. Boy, were they ever wrong! There were no words of encouragement on any level from these people. I think about people like this all the time and I have to smile. My main reason for smiling in the face of the "N" word is because I have the knowledge that let me know, I don't have to bow down, or be discouraged by negativity. I'm always as strong as I allow myself to be and with that strength my FOCUS remains clear. Every negative block you step on, becomes a stepping-stone to success.

Living your life T.O.T.B. and BOTAAE takes courage. There will be encouragement on the positive side and a lack of encouragement on the negative side. The word "encouragement" used in this chapter has both a positive and a negative connotation, but in each instance of encouragement, "COURAGE" always prevails. When you allow yourself to be open to any and everything, some people who may not understand your FOCUS might think you are slightly different or a little out there. They might think you've lost what little mind you have left. I look at it this way, "you're damned if you do and damned if you don't, so I think I'd rather be damned doing something positive with my life." Bringing some of the ideas or memories stored in your box to the surface is what we are here to do. Think about it… if you allow yourself to be open to the world around you, you may begin to live life again or see the possibility of a better life and future for you and your family. The way you lived your life when you were a child, naive enough to believe you could do any and everything! Living without boundaries is what allows you to enter the deepest recesses of your mind because this is where dreams are formed and begin to manifest. What do you have to lose, but the dreams in your spirit if you don't? If you lose the dreams, then you lose the vision. We don't get much time on the planet so; wasted time for anyone could mean lost opportunities. Allowing yourself to be that open person, gives you the ability to experience many special moments and in some of those special moments, you will begin to understand your point and purpose in life.

BOTAAE is a key building block of FOCUS. When you wake up in the morning and take that daily look in the mirror, can you tell me what you see? Are you seeing your life's full potential? You should be! Are you seeing opportunities around every corner? Why not? Finally, are you sure you want to take the journey down this road? You really should be! A reminder for you… fear is always present, but it is not an option to accept anymore. Learn to use the fear in any situation as motivation not to give up. Because you have choices you have the right to keep a positive mindset and you also have the right to believe in yourself. Being outside the box, fear in the past would've caused you to shut down. Now you can spring forward with determination and courage to drive the life you live. BOTAAE takes a lot more courage than you might understand right now, but the courage needed is inside you waiting to get out. I mentioned courage to you earlier in an example of positive and negative so let's take a look at the word "COURAGE."

Courage is a noun and it is defined as…
1) Courage: The quality of being brave, valor
2) Courage: Bravery, valor, boldness, fearlessness, spirit.

Look at courage and how it relates to your life. Do you have the courage necessary to make the positive changes in your life? I hope you believe this is a new day. Learning BOTAAE creates an openness allowing you to begin to breathe. During my law enforcement career, I did many things during my service that could have been considered courageous, but I just looked at it as doing my job. I'd also like to think I put in the time through my life, training and experience in law enforcement, to make the right decisions. I'd also like to believe the inner strength you possess would come out when it has to. Looking back as I think about courage in most cases and for most people it is always thinking outside the box, but you have to be open and willing, in order to do anything that would put others before you. BOTAAE will become second nature as your FOCUS and Clarity come into view and so will the life you dreamed for yourself. It's like this… opportunities are and have always been present. You didn't know that because your vision was clouded. Living BOTAAE will allow you to discover your true life, outside the Matrix. The world you live in will one day be exposed for it's true value. The world we live in is all we have and as you learn to make the most of everyday, that's when you'll start to really, live. One day I came to a realization about my life. I realized the value I placed on, or gave my life and the lives of the people close to me was not only important to me, but it was the only way I could see living my life to the fullest. I learned to live life, and not just to hang around waiting to die! My second chance allowed me a better understanding of BOTAAE and that gave me the joy I live with today. It also allowed me to understand if I'm alive I can always put in the work to make things better in my environment.

I told you earlier I was born on June 7, 1960 and because I was born in the early part of June, so astrologically I am considered a Gemini, The Twins. The third sign of the zodiac and being a twin, I have to share my life with my other side on a regular basis. I'm not a real zodiac chart person, but I do believe we all have two sides that are in a constant battle with one another. There is what we choose to do with our lives and the all-important what we have to do. It's taken a little time but I've learned to do both. As I earned a living in law enforcement and personal security, I prepared myself to become a writer. Even though fear kept coming to the forefront, I still worked at creating this future for myself. Don't get angry or upset about it, learn to FOCUS to understand and accept that you are able to do more than you think. If you're BOTAAE identify the other side exists and work on learning to control it, or learn to let it out. Gemini or not, we are all faced with the same battles. The inner struggles we face will be with us as long as we live and with some of us even after we die. All kidding aside, we do have to get used to double duty. Do I go left or right? Do I say yes or no? Do I take this job or that job? These are just some of the questions that must be answered. Believe it or not, when I say, "We have to live our lives with those two sides," that's just a metaphor as to how our brains work. The strength of mind that is crucial in the development of our Soul Step plays a major role in the path you choose. Looking at the world and BOTAAE does not mean you have to go out every day and try to save it; it also does not mean you have to try and have an answer, to every situation that pops up. BOTAAE is all about choices and being able, or in a position to understand what's in front of you and why it's there. Why are things positive or negative happening, and how do I respond when they do?

LIFEWORK JOURNAL ENTRY

The path or journey we take in life is determined in every way by BOTAAE. Whether we realize it or not, most of the decisions we make are based on the limited or unlimited circumstances surrounding our lives. BOTAAE is learning to live beyond your limits. Some have a hard time BOTAAE when they can't see a physical future. Sometimes it takes a person hitting rock bottom before they open their spirit to see a brighter future, or to find their true purpose or ability. As a kid growing up in Compton, not joining a gang was one of the choices I have to believe saved my life! During that time in Compton, it appeared as though the gangs had all the power in the hood and I have to admit it was a little enticing, but I held fast to my convictions so I would not ever be in the position to be convicted! The courage that lived inside me at the time developed the strength necessary for me to continue to be an individual. I've said this before about standing alone. It is not easy, but you have to be up and open to the challenge. You also have to remember challenges are an integral part of your life, that says everything happens in your life the way it's supposed to. They are a part of your growth and development, but they also accompany every opportunity. The vision it takes to work toward the goals you have set are astronomical. Consistent hard work to step up and face every challenge allows you the openness necessary to "EMBRACE" every challenge. I've learned it's not going to be easy, so get ready to meet these challenges, head on, with the courage to maintain a positive attitude. Like I said before, there are something's you just have to go through.

END LIFEWORK JOURNAL ENTRY

As I grew older I began to clearly see and understand the choices I made, based on BOTAAE would be with me for the rest of my life and I have to think they were great choices. Going through everything I went through allowed me to develop a great deal of respect for myself and for the people I came in contact with. That respect I developed allowed me to see the so-called cleaning lady and President Barrack Obama in the same light, "HUMAN BEING!" From the guy who bags my groceries at the market, to Warren Buffett, or any other CEO of every Fortune 500 Company, they have to be treated as equals and with the same level of respect. "HUMAN BEING!" The human factor has to always be first. No matter what someone does or says, they are a person first. We should never judge anyone by the circumstances they live in or what they do for a living. As people, we are in many cases more than what our outward appearance, race, creed, color, status, male, female or the jobs we hold in this society. Wisdom can come to you when you least expect it. If you allow yourself to be open to this, the Universe is wide open and ripe for the picking.

Let's get back to that two-headed monster we have to deal with, the sharing of the two sides within. I have discovered they will always be in conflict with one another, but the key to managing the positive side of your Soul Step is FOCUS. The more on the positive side you choose to live your life the more negativity will attempt to enter in. The good thing about the positive side of your Soul Step is, eventually it will take over. Even though the "N" word will always try and creep in and disrupt your flow, it won't succeed. Remember the word fortitude? Well if you don't it's back! Fortitude is the strength of mind that develops in plotting a course to success and guess what? Clarity will and is meant to grow! If I may refer back to the Matrix, looking at what is really in front of you, BOTAAE will become one of those keys I spoke about earlier. It's an awareness that creates a sixth sense, helping you to see every detail of your life in a better light, so you don't continue to live the circumstances that is your current environment. Having the keys to success and not being able to identify the doors will no longer exist. It's almost like being able to understand how a magician's trick works. BOTAAE will not only help you to find the doors it will also help you identify which doors should be opened and which doors you should walk away from. Learning to walk away from some of the doors placed before you are sometimes the hardest thing to do, but at times it will be extremely necessary. You'll learn most importantly to listen to your spirit before, during and after you make decisions. There's a phrase that goes "Let your conscience be your guide," that's your spirit trying to help you to navigate your steps and move in the right direction. As you move through each day, the five clarities will become extremely important, as you evaluate each situation. In chapter four, I told you as you evaluate the people in your life, sometimes you might have to shed the negative ones. Knowing when to walk away and being able to do it can be extremely difficult, but sometimes you have to think about yourself and living a better and stress-free life. You may not be able to have a completely stress-free life, but you can control and minimize the amount of stress you take in from the people in your life. I also hope you remember I did not say cut everyone away, but in your evaluation it's about a better quality of life. BOTAAE will help you to remove ego from the decisions you make. If you have to make some decisions and you realize the only way to move forward in some situations is to ask for help, then please by all means ask. Ego will always resist asking or looking to others for help. Men know that all too well! I learned to reject ego when I was a Deputy Sheriff. I discovered early on, "EGO" would get you killed in the streets! Having a partner in the field or knowing you have back up is a key to surviving in the streets as a Deputy Sheriff and it is also key component to surviving in life. Again, it's called help! Another key to FOCUS is to know at some time in your life, you're going to need and also give help. I just want you to maintain your FOCUS and don't allow anyone that is not there to help you cloud your vision and distract you from your goals. The FOCUS that our lives are based on is the true, clearer reality we have to live beyond. Your Soul Step should be filled with the same PDD that has been inside you from the time you're born. When we are children we have dreams and ideas, some fantasy, but they are a reality to us. When children want to be something, it doesn't matter what circumstance you grew up in, or where you grew up for that matter, you had those dreams. I remember as a child my parents told me I could be anything in this world that I wanted to be. They even told me that one day if I wanted to I could be President. I loved my parents with everything in me, but I knew deep down in my spirit I never wanted to be President. I wanted to be a writer! I never thought I would see a "BLACK PRESIDENT" in my lifetime. Boy was I ever wrong! President Barack Obama changed the course of American history and with President Obama becoming the first black President, serving two terms

I believe there is nothing I can't do. NOTHING! I guess that is truly BOTAAE… wow I could even be President if I chose to put in the work.

Growing up we sometimes lose sight of our childhood dreams. As children we sometimes have the most abstract thoughts and our thinking was always outside the box. Why do you think that is? As children, I believe we want to be and do everything that passes through our spirit. These ideas and or thoughts are placed in our spirits to be used at a later date. We keep most of them as memories stored in our box. Good and bad they are there and fortunately one day we can draw from them, learn to FOCUS and create the future we want, love and desire for ourselves. At times my parents didn't understand me and may have thought I was even a little weird, or often times crazy! Through it all they loved me no matter what decisions I made. Unfortunately, most parents can be locked in and caught in the Matrix. I can understand as a parent looking at many children today and even my own children and think they may be a little strange… but children live outside the box and they believe in themselves, until someone tells them too many times they can't do something. I understand how they feel because I am that child. I say they're a little strange only because, I live outside that same box and I also know how it feels to dream. Because of FOCUS, I won't allow anyone to stop the dreams I hold in my heart. As we mature, we lose the fearlessness we had as children that allowed us to dream without fear. When we were young children many of us believed there was nothing we wouldn't try or there was nothing we could not do. If we fell down, hurt or not we would jump up like it never happened and continued to play. As time passes, we lose that openness to try anything new. Now when we fall we may not get up as quickly, but we do get up! Sometimes we become products in the system of "I CAN'T" because we've been told that so many times, we begin to believe it, so we start living it. You have to rediscover that sense of adventure again. Don't get all hot, bothered and angry! I'm not saying not to be smart… you should always proceed with caution, but anything you decide to do, please do your homework first. Knowledge will create an inner strength, giving you the ability of Being Open To Any And Everything. (YOU HAVE TO GET UP!)

LIFEWORK JOURNAL ENTRY

In chapter one I told you about some of the things I have done in my life and one of those things is holding several patents, with several business partners on fitness equipment we designed. Being a creative person, I can truly say I woke-up one morning with an idea or two in my brain and with the assistance of partners (HELP) we were able to design and build this equipment. Because of the creative process this portion of the work was easy and now we move to the hard part. How do we go about filing for a patent and what would this process cost? How long would it take before the patent was granted and what about this and what about that and what about everything??? Man did we have our work cut out for us. During the study process of finding out how to get this patent I learned patent attorneys are extremely intelligent. They are true specialist in this field of study because most patent attorneys start out as some sort of engineer and then they become an attorney. Can you imagine? I also found out patent attorneys are extremely passionate about their work so I have to believe that their PDD levels are through the roof! A patent attorney's Soul Step walks into the room days before he even thinks about walking in. I believe they are the true "Rock Stars" of the legal world. One of the points I am trying to make is without the help of this very unique person we would not have been able to protect all of the hard work we put into our product design and development. The second thing I want you to understand is, the study I put into place when I met with this patent attorney and the knowledge I acquired in this process, will be with me for the rest of my life. Let's get back to those dreams…

END LIFEWORK JOURNAL ENTRY

Once we lose our dreams some of us slowly lose the Passion, Drive and Desire that is still living in our DNA. (YOU HAVE TO GET UP!) Sometimes we need a jumpstart and I want Unlikely Destiny Volume One, to be that jumpstart. BOTAAE plays a major role in bringing the fearlessness back to the surface. If you can think back about some of the crazy things you did as a child, because you didn't know any better or were fearless, you didn't care what your peers thought about you, so you at least tried. Rarely did you ever think about giving up because in many cases as children we don't understand that concept until it becomes a learned behavior. In fact, if you think about it sometimes the more out their things were, the harder you tried, at least I did. Sometimes the more effort you put into anything, the more attention you received. Sometimes that attention was positive and other times it became negative. They may not have said anything but as they got older their respect for you in most cases grew. Or they became jealous in either case you were always fearless. As a child you took chances good, bad or otherwise… you were open to almost everything, right? Well it's time to get back to understanding the child you were and the dreams you had. If you had these dreams once, they are still inside you, and you just have to dig deep and let them flow. (CLARITY IN MEMORY) One of the best things about getting older and knowing what you know, is that you don't have to place limits on your life or the lives of the people you meet. One of the many lessons I hope you learn from Unlikely Destiny is you can work on your dreams, goals and most of all your aspirations. You can change your circumstance thus creating a new outlook on your environment and our Universe. Think about this for a minute… everything, every idea, every thought, every vision, every memory, every person, every situation, every day, every meeting, I could keep doing this for a while… I want you to understand it has all been placed before you for, "YOU!" You have to get back to living your dreams and stop worrying about what those around you may think. Who cares what these idiots think? Anybody can give up! We see people do it every day, but not you because you're not a quitter or a loser. You are focused and directed in your life and nothing will be able to stop you from meeting every goal period! If you dig deep and find you don't have any dreams right now, then I suggest you refer back to "Chapter Two". Go stand back in the mirror, look a little longer and go a little deeper within yourself. There has to be something that continues to burn inside you on some level and if you take the time and recognize the light, you should see your dreams, goals and aspirations coming back into FOCUS.

I spent many years thinking about writing a book, writing this book. I spent years looking for that light at the end of the tunnel. I saw flashes of light here and there, but nothing held my interest like writing. Even though I knew I wanted to write, I still had some doubts in the back of my mind about my abilities. I finally discovered my search for the light I was looking for was inside me all the time. I'm telling you if a fire is burning in your spirit, it will never die! Ignoring it in many cases will make the fire burn with more intensity. BOTAAE will always start within, because you are not only a light for yourself, you will become a light for everyone you meet. You have to always think about the future. People always laugh when the conversation comes up about staying away from the light… stay away from the light! I've always believed everything will come to light in due time so that's where we need to go. We need to open our eyes and our hearts, so we can summon our inner strength, that inner light. The Universe is the light that will shine brighter than any star in the heavens. This light gives us the strength that we will be able pull from in our time of need. I have mentioned the Universe several times already in this book and believe me, I will use it again. I'm not sure if you're aware of the vastness of our Universe so let's take a look at the definition of Universe:

Universe is a noun and it is defined as…

1) The totality of all matter and energy that exist in the vastness of space, whether known to human beings or not.
2) The Earth along with the human race and the totality of the human experience.

The totality of all matter and energy, talk about BOTAAE! You have to believe you belong to something much bigger than you. Believing that "yes, you matter" and not only do you matter, but you also have a strong place in the Universe, has to give you a sense of inner peace and excitement at the same time. That is what I like to call, "Focus Forward Energy." What we do on every level affects our Universe! The Universe we all occupy space in needs you always at your best to help create the balance necessary for our existence. The energy of matter that makes us, should give you an idea that we are unique in our existence and as you look at this life remember; "If we are in the Universe, the Universe is in us." The point is, the vastness of our Universe dwells inside each of us and because it does, it means we have the space and capacity inside to grow, thereby creating endless possibilities. Please tell me you're thinking about what you just read? On every level we have the capacity for growth and development beyond what we see and presently live! Keeping this really simple… every great person started as a baby, grew up in some neighborhood, had a mother and a father and at some point, in their lives someone recognized they had a point and purpose. This is when they began BOTAAE and the Universe of endless possibilities is now open. Ultimately, we change our mindset, by believing there are no limits. When you stop and think about your life remember it's your life to live. As you live it BOTAAE will not only help you to move Focus Forward, you will be able to see everything in real time, Clarity in Vision. Every dream, every idea, every goal, every aspiration, from the time you were born, are inside you, like a loaded computer's hard drive (Clarity in Memory). As we grow into our lives we have a tendency to sometimes lose faith in ourselves and in our dreams. (YOU HAVE TO GET UP!) At times some of us just flat out give up on the life we wanted for our ourselves and our families. If you don't get anything from this book my wish is that you take a step back, look at your life then dare to dream again. If I could explain BOTAAE I would say don't ever lose sight of the vision in your dreams. Think about the life you are living and know that "YOU" can make it better. I don't care if you think you have everything you need… always think about helping someone else!

LIFEWORK JOURNAL ENTRY

I have been extremely blessed in my life… because of the jobs I've had, the people I've had the privilege to work for and with, my life has been amazing! I believe BOTAAE is the number one reason for every bit of my success. Growing up where I grew up, the only way I could see my future was when I began to believe everything is possible. I didn't know what my success would be at the time, but even in my sometimes-negative state of mind as a child, I still had an open mind, which created an optimistic future. I began to believe there wasn't anything that I wanted to do, that would not get done. I knew one day I would travel and I have been to many countries around the world. I have also been to every major city, in every state, in the United States and most of them more than once. Lastly, I am also fortunate enough to have been born and raised in southern California and I have had the opportunity to live in New York City for the past twenty plus years. As much as I didn't want to live in "The Big Apple" I was open to it. BOTAAE has opened many doors in my life and I'm forever grateful and I know for a fact that BOTAAE also helped to keep me out of the gangs, it allowed me to see beyond my neighborhood and it gave me the positive mindset I live with today. (YOU HAVE TO GET UP!)

END LIFEWORK JOURNAL ENTRY

Allowing yourself to be open to the Universe could provide life changes that could propel you forward enhancing your everyday existence. Many of us believe the Universe is filled with mystery and we are fascinated with that mystery… we need to look at our lives in the same manner. Learn to be fascinated with your existence, but remove the mystery by BOTAAE. Learn to enjoy the journey, good and bad. We are amazing beings on this planet, and our individual lives are seamless, but by working together in the positive, we can become unbeatable. Unfortunately, and fortunately, as individuals there are three things in life, we all of have to go through for mental, spiritual, and physical growth. From time to time we will be pushed beyond what we believe are the normal limits of our existence. These limits are something we all must experience… "Anger, Depression, To Enlightenment." **(YOU HAVE TO GET UP!)**

7

Three Steps In Life You Must Go Through... Anger, Depression, To Enlightenment

Only if you have been in the deepest valley can you ever know how magnificent it is to be on the highest mountain...

Richard M. Nixon

<u>**STEP ONE ANGER:**</u>

Anger is a noun and is defined as
1) A feeling of extreme annoyance.
2) To become or make somebody extremely annoyed!

I spoke earlier about going through crap and learning from your experiences, but if you remember I also said learning from someone else's experiences is a better way to learn. Trust me it is better to learn from someone else's experiences, but this time, in this chapter, you have to go through this yourself. This chapter will be a larger dose of self-reflection as a means to a better understanding of you.

Anger is how it starts! I want you to go back and look at the definition of anger and read it several times. Like my Dad says to me "Meditate on it for little while and let it get down into your spirit." If you're angry right now, this chapter will help you through to the positive side of your Soul Step. If you're not angry I'm sure you can remember the feeling anger brings out in you. I want you to recall that feeling without continuing to live there. The reason I say, "Not to live there," when you think about anger there are some people you know, who live their lives in a state of anger twenty-four, seven. They have never looked to change. As you meditate on "ANGER" don't let it get into your spirit, but you need a complete understanding of this definition to help you evolve to Enlightenment. There was a time I thought anger was an okay place to live and while living in this angry state, I believed it was normal. I believed most people lived most of their lives angry, because that's what I saw in my environment everyday growing up. Even when I moved to New York, I felt like everyone I passed on the street was angry. That was so far from the truth it's not even funny. There is nothing funny about living in anger and defeat, but if we learn to dig deep we will be able to find a little humor in some of the reasons we got angry in the past (CLARITY IN MEMORY). Clarity in memory is crucial in dealing with your internal anger. Anger is a noun and nouns are a person, place or thing, but in this case, anger is a thing, or is it a place? Or could it be a person? Anger can be all three and you really need to be careful when you encounter it on any level. For all intents and purposes, we will place anger in the category of being a thing. Giving anger a place gives it tangibility, thereby making it as real as the food you eat or the car you drive. I'd like to take the "person and place" away from anger in order to keep it as a thing. People and places can be physically moved away from on some level, but if it's a "thing", it gives us the opportunity to put something in its place. Not in our box keeping our spirit clutter free. Everything in life has at least two sides and I believe there are positive and negative sides to everything including "ANGER." The positive side to anger if used properly, can help you FOCUS on goals allowing you to meet those goals with strength, direction and purpose. We need to work on understanding how anger works in our lives and as we understand our anger, I believe this, will give us a much better understanding of ourselves. Controlling your anger with direction is optimum in maintaining FOCUS and clarity during difficult situations.

Looking at my life, there were a number of reasons I could have been angry and in reality, for a number of years I was! I was angry about where I grew up, because I knew there were better places to live. I was also angry with the gangs in my neighborhood, because of the danger they produced! Anger, is only one letter short of "DANGER!" Because of the environment I grew up in anger became a learned behavior, thereby creating a never-ending cycle of negative circumstances to live down too. In a fit of anger many people, myself included, have made poor choices that could be considered dangerous. If allowed, anger can chip away at what makes us human and create something our own family won't even recognize. According to the information site, Answers.com "Anger, is a chemical response that affects the whole body, it is brought on by simple thoughts, that are usually fear based, the root of thought, is a fear of losing something or someone." The main problem with anger is the chemical rush, created by the brain clouding rational thought. Someone who is angry is usually focused with a narrow view and can't see the whole picture. Anger is probably the main cause of death on the planet (WARS, RIOTS, ACTING ON IMPULSE, JEALOUSY, SUICIDE BOMBING, or SUICIDE etc.) Anger doesn't have to destroy you... I realized it was going to be a part of my life, a part of our lives, whether we wanted it to be or not, but we don't have to react to it in a negative manner. Because most of us have experienced periods of anger, those moments have been stored in our memories (Clarity in Memory). The anger that has been stored in our memories in many cases can be "TRIGGERED" by specific incidents in our lives i.e. places, smells, words, but in most cases its people. Some of the people in our lives know just how to trip the triggers that send us into an angry rage!

Anger is defined as, a feeling of extreme annoyance, but it can also be an "EXTREME EMOTION" that could drive you insane, if the energy it produces is not pushed in the right direction. Let's take a step back and look at the word "Extreme."

Extreme is an adjective and it is defined as:
1) Highest in intensity or degree
2) Going far beyond what is reasonable or normal

There is an "EXTREME EMOTION" burning deep inside my spirit that releases the anger of every day I felt cheated in life, every person I've lost to death, drugs or jail, every situation I've been in and felt helpless, every time I believed my mother did not want me, which I would later find out was the deepest root of my anger. My anger has now been released into the world to run amuck. Now growing up where I grew up, just because I didn't get caught up in gangs, drugs, or any of the other negative pitfalls that presented themselves to me, doesn't mean I wasn't affected and my world didn't go through more changes than the weather. If you are human and have an ounce of love in your heart, you can't help being angry about the negative things that happen to you and around you. It took a lot of work for me not to allow anger to consume my life or continue to control my daily steps. I had to figure out a way to make anger an unlearned behavior, even though it was deeply rooted in my spirit, because of what I believed and the environment I was born into. I have a mantra that I learned to say to myself on a regular basis, "Live it! Love it! Accept it"! Live your life, love your life and the sooner you accept you have a hand in the direction your life takes, by the work you're willing to put in, the sooner you can implement change. The only way you'll be able to do any of this is learning to control this thing called "ANGER." Anger can't be swept under a rug or put on hold. You can't treat anger with a single bandage if it's spewing from more than a single place. Anger is a cancer that must be treated in order for you to maintain control over it, or cut it out completely. Anger if focused properly can help you, but if not controlled it can truly hurt you, but your reaction through free will, is always up to you. What brings out my anger? I had several triggers in the past bringing out the worst in me, but over the past twenty-plus years I've learned to control those triggers, with what I use as my, "THREE LEVELS OF CONTROL."

THE FIRST LEVEL OF CONTROL
"NOT ALLOWING ANYTHING I CAN'T
CONTROL, TO CONTROL ME"

As infants and children anger is not something we are born with. As infants and even as young children we will go to anyone we meet. No matter what their race, creed, color, straight, gay, dog, cat or bat, we are all like little sponges absorbing anything given to us. Unfortunately, anger is one of the legacies that is passed on to our children because it was passed on to us. My belief, anger is a learned behavior that is logged and stored in our spirit and unfortunately it gets locked in our box as a memory. Anger, becoming a memory can come out whenever we want it to, or when it's triggered. Because we've learned to hold on to it, it's a crutch we carry at times with pride and honor, because we believe anger is not only necessary, it's essential to our survival. I've seen anger first hand as a child, a teenager, an adult, as a Deputy Sheriff, an Inglewood Police Officer and more times than I care to recall in my personal life. I believe anger is mostly expressed through ignorance, fear and a lack of belief or faith in yourself. If you don't get anything out of the anger portion of this chapter please get this, "YOU CAN'T CONTROL THE ACTIONS AND WHAT OTHER PEOPLE DO." Meditate on that for a minute or two. This may sound crazy but, in the thirty plus years between my law enforcement career and personal security, dealing with the anger of others, has taught me to understand and deal with my own anger issues. My job became a blessing in disguise on so many levels. When you have to work through any anger issues of two or more people, it affords you the opportunity to see every side of each person's point of view. It taught me to be impartial and far removed from judging others. FOCUS allowed me to see, the sooner you mentally rebound from something that triggered your anger, the sooner you can get back on track, maintain your FOCUS and continue seeing opportunities that present themselves to you. If you live in "ANGER" on a daily basis, the anger you project creates a barrier or a force field if you will, that deflects every positive thought you could ever wish to have. By releasing anger from your box, this could keep you from growing beyond the circumstances that are plaguing your environment. I've learned over time to keep life simple by understanding if something happened, no matter how devastating, it can't be taken back. For example, the angry outburst I had with my sister's, Debbie and Mara. I can never take back the anger I displayed that day because it has been logged away word for word in their spirit and locked in their box. Even though they have both long since forgiven me, anger often creates unique scars on the hearts of people we love. The e-mail you wrote to someone during a bout of anger once you push the send button, that negative energy you created is on its way to creating another scar somewhere in your environment. I have this belief that our family and friends, who live in our environment, often create the most unique scars on our lives. These scars we create can and will heal, but a scar is still a scar. If that happens too many times, with too many of the people we love, one day they'll lose faith in us, causing us to lose faith in ourselves, creating fear which will eventually lead back to triggering anger. This could create a domino effect not allowing our abilities to grow or develop to their full potential and the perpetual motion of anger will continue and you are the one who loses in the end. Too much loss has a tendency to create a mindset and a lifestyle that could push you to even higher levels of this insidious disease. To me anger is a disease, like cancer or heart disease! It builds up over time and can kill you slowly or it could strike hard and fast like a heart attack. Bottom line anger can destroy everything in its path, from people to entire countries. It also creates a loss. A loss for you and everyone you meet. Take a minute and look at every morning you wake up, just waking up today you have the opportunity to create a better day than yesterday, but most people don't look at their lives that way. This is how we start our day "Focus Forward." In most cases if you go to sleep with anger in your heart, it's had all night to fester and you'll wake up with the same anger intensified. If you have an argument with your wife or your children and create a frustrating morning, this could be just one of the triggers out of several thousand that could bring anger to the surface. I've been there, you've been there, we've all had one or two "Morning Triggers" (M.T.) that has ruined our day, and the day of everyone we come in contact with, after we leave our cave. In situations where anger has been triggered, my mindset goes immediately to; "Is this what I want the last conversation to be with someone I love?" The answer for that will always be "NO!" This works for me to bring me back to my reality so to speak. Nothing says you will return home at the end of each day. We pray hoping we do return home safely, but every day some of us leave home never to return. During my law enforcement career and in the world of personal security, the thought of not returning home at the "end of watch" has crossed my mind more than once. It's a reality of the job, we as security professionals know going in. The thing about anger in the streets could get you injured or killed if you lose FOCUS in the performance of your duties. As a deputy sheriff and a police officer, I have made several "Death Notifications" to the next of kin, a parent and even the children of parents and in several of these instances their final words to one another were said in "Extreme Anger!" Now you have to live through this situation, the mental and spiritual anguish you have to bare can leave you without any hope in your immediate future.

What can you control in your environment? You can control what you do, or how you react to every situation. You can control what you say, but most of all you can always control how you decide to treat everyone. Keeping the human factor always in the front of my mind keeps me in check and my anger locked in the right box. Everyone handles and deals with stress, which is a major trigger for anger in different ways. In most cases things said in anger, from one person to another are mostly said to hurt the other person because that person is hurting for one reason or another. When anger is pushed in my direction I've learned to look at the human side of the equation, to try and understand just where their anger is coming from. I think to myself, "You never know what the other person is going through." This keeps me in check, thereby cooling what would be my anger, not clouding my judgment, there-by allowing me the ability to see every piece of the puzzle. I've had the opportunity to practice this technique many times over the years. I know for a fact each time I could have allowed my anger to be triggered and released, I was able to suppress the urge and maintained control over the situation. This has created a much stronger FOCUS in me and positive relationships are maintained. Now understand this, I never let anyone or any situation take advantage of me. I am strong in the person I have become and no one can ever take that away from me. It's the same as acquired knowledge, once you have it, it will always be yours.

LIFE WORK JOURNAL ENTRY

Since more than half of my adult life was dedicated to law enforcement, I've experienced anger and I've had anger directed at me because of the uniform. I said before that anger is a learned behavior. As a kid growing up in Watts and Compton we were taught by our peers, The Black Panthers and some adults in our neighborhood, not to like or trust Compton P.D., LAPD or the L.A. County Sheriff's. Anytime we were approached by anyone in law enforcement they were met with pseudo-anger and pseudo-anger, because there was no real reason for us to feel this way. Even if they were there to help us, we accepted their help, but we still met them with our pseudo-anger in gratitude. Now the anger I received as a law enforcement officer was the same that I dished out as a kid. Because I know the root and the base of this anger, I was able to meet it with an understanding and FOCUS, which allowed me to resist meeting pseudo-anger, with any anger at all. The point of this exercise in anger is to show that this learned behavior can be controlled. I've learned to control my anger by learning its root and most importantly controlling how I react to the triggers. Knowing my mother really did love me created a wellness in my heart that began the process of healing my spirit, thereby allowing me to change my world.

END LIFEWORK JOURNAL ENTRY

Your anger, just like everything else in your life, has as much energy and control, as you chose to give it. Anger has a tendency to create chaos leaving everyone and everything in its path un-focused! Losing FOCUS can cause you to miss out on opportunities that have your name written all over them. FOCUS keeps you relevant, FOCUS keeps you in the moment, FOCUS allows you a logical answer to many of the questions you have in the back of your mind. I believe we have the keys to success embedded deep in our spirit, but success, just like everything is different for everyone. Anger deflects, detracts, and in some cases destroys ambition, if not controlled. Anger can keep you from living the life of your dreams or the life in your spirit. Controlling anger is the best way to keep it from controlling you or your environment. Anger can be turned into passion and your "PASSION" is fuel for the "DRIVE" and "DESIRE" that is deeply rooted in your spirit, needed and used to accomplish our goals.

THE SECOND LEVEL OF CONTROL
"HOW DOES WHAT'S HAPPENING
AFFECT MY ENVIRONMENT?"

There are several reasons or ways anger may affect our environment, and in many cases create a world for us that has no direction. This is all created by situations, which lead to circumstances, people, and bad decisions that are all brought about in most cases by us. That's right, most of what goes on with us, is because of our actions or lack thereof, causing us to be angry or live in an angry state, and this angry state creates a new and unimproved environment. The anger that develops because of what we do is an entirely different animal of the anger tree. This anger as it relates to us is the psychological threat creating our own private Matrix. Living your life in a state of anger is the environment you develop, because of some of your decisions. Now hear me when I say "some of your decisions." I'm saying "some," because I grew up in an environment that could have, and should have created many bad situations, but this doesn't mean I had to conform to those circumstances. Temptation, peer pressure and a whole host of situations will many times scream in your face, calling out your name but, free will gives you the right to say "Yes" or "No." I'm not saying every decision you make that doesn't work out how you hoped it would, is a bad decision. We will have more failures than successes, but it's those who rebound on the positive side of every situation, that will determine who will survive by maintaining their FOCUS. The same way you are responsible for your "box" you are responsible for the environment you create. If you find yourself in a world of constant confusion and dysfunction this could make anyone angry, but it will also keep you from reaching your intended goals or dreams. For years my environment was a resting place for anger. The space I lived in mentally and physically, was plagued with confusion and dysfunction along with my own list of internal struggles. Some of our internal struggles may never fully go away. They could be locked in your box until the day you die, so you may as well learn to live a happy and fruitful life in spite of your struggles. Now I'm not saying give in or give up, but recognizing where you are in life should give you the motivation to look for a better way to live. My mindset says, "To struggle is to be challenged," and how we respond to challenges are what make us who we hope to one day become... Successful!

We have all experienced things in our childhood and or those crazy teenage years, that will continue to live in our box and pop out every now and again, that's a given. Like I said before, it has already happened! We can't change our past, but we can change our future by how we react to our past. By living in the "NOW" that keeps our Soul Step, always Focus Forward. Most of us have lived through one or two devastating events that rocked our

Soul Step like no other, but we learn through these challenges that we are strong and we can make the choice to accept a better way of life. If you find that certain people or certain situations are creating stress, in almost every case this can lead to anger. Well you know what that means? Changing your environment could mean re-evaluating some of your relationships. I have found the older and wiser I've gotten, the less I will allow anyone or anything to upset the balance in the life I've created. I've also learned to keep everything in my life as simple as possible. If keeping your anger under wraps means some people have to go, then they will have to go. Bottom line to this is, every time you're distracted from working toward your goals or lifelong dreams, you're not allowing yourself to take advantage of "your" opportunities. You need to understand your environment is you and every person you decide to bring along for the ride, is going to affect the outcome of everything you do.

If your anger causes you to lose clarity in every area of your life, you will never be able to grow. Anger can stunt your mental, spiritual, and in many cases, your environmental growth. There's a saying "the company you keep," and ninety-nine percent of the time it is only said when something bad or negative happens. I wonder what happens when you surround yourself with people who have positive attitudes that lead to positive actions, creating a positive environment? Seriously I want you to think about your life and where you are and if you can't come up with at least one positive for every negative then you have some work to do! You have to find a way to keep balance in your life. This is something you need to look at and log in your "LIFEWORK JOURNAL." Balance is extremely important in everything we do, so I like to try and always apply a Yin and Yang approach to my life. Anger exists in our environment believe it or not to bring it balance. According to Newton's Law of Motion, everything that exists has an equal or opposite reaction. The word "anger" has several opposites that can create the balance necessary for it to exist. The three I like most for Unlikely Destiny are Love, Peace, and Self Control. Developing these three, what I would call "Disciplines," are an effective tool to combat anger in order to control your environment. I said it before, anger is not ever going away, but it is treatable and, in some cases, can be cured, like any other disease. Because anger is a learned behavior it can be treated with love, peace, and self-control.

All three of these disciplines alone have their own power; the power of love, peace be unto you all and the development of your self-control is a blessing you will come to understand with daily practice. Another aid to help develop these disciplines is the self-reflection you do in the mirror every day. The mirror allows you to look at the anger attempting to hide behind your eyes deep in your spirit. Seeing anger and not hiding it lets you deal with everything in your environment at your own pace, so you're not overwhelmed. Every day you mirror you break down anger, piece by piece giving you the ability to take control of it.

Many of us are born into situations that were created by many before us, but never the less now we are here. Anger fills this cup and without thinking we drink from it every day. There will come a day when we reach a certain age or we experience a spiritual awakening that we decide (which free will allows us too) to stop drinking from this cup of anger. I did! As our clarity begins getting clearer, we begin to see opportunities that have been placed before us, allowing our FOCUS to continue forward always in a positive mode. If you're focused on accomplishing your goals even during the most frustrating parts of what you're doing, this will help to keep anger at bay. We begin to fight back and fight for a better existence that will allow us the opportunity to make a better world for ourselves. We begin to meet pseudo-anger head on stopping it before it can disrupt our positive flow. Where you live both mentally and spiritually is completely up to you. The next time you feel anger begin to rear its ugly head in your mind, body and spirit, THINK! Think about where the anger is truly coming from. Think about your reaction and how your anger will affect your present and your future. The bottom line is I just want you to "THINK FIRST"! Thinking through all the areas of your anger is the most effective way to gain control of anger. The environment you learn to create will come through being honest with yourself. Allowing like-minded people to become a blessing and sharing in your life, will feed your spirit with the right nourishment for, whatever it is you're doing. This will help to put the control of anger in your hands.

THE THIRD LEVEL OF CONTROL
"ARE WE CURING CANCER IN THIS SITUATION?"

I told you earlier, I believe stress is one of the biggest causes for anger. My third level of controlling anger is asking myself several times a day "ARE WE CURING CANCER IN THIS SITUATION?" It is my way of keeping anger in perspective as it relates to a particular situation. Ninety percent of the situations that create my anger can be squashed with this phrase, just by thinking it too myself.

Prior to being able to FOCUS and understanding the base of anger, I didn't think this way. I would meet anger with anger and I gave it just as well as anyone could. I have been blessed enough to grow beyond the anger that kept me from being able to see opportunities that were placed before me. Every day we are faced with situations that can make us grow as people or cause us to shrink and give into the stress that creates our anger. We have to go through crap in order to develop ways of dealing with the stress that creates our anger. Trial and error will become our own personal "double blind" study into ourselves. For most of us as we deal with or assimilate stress over time we become proficient at handling it. We are able to then learn how to control anger one situation at a time. My acronym for "CRAAP": Creating Real And Active Possibilities is another technique I use to keep anger at bay. Every day is not going to be easy or go according to plan if you are out trying to make your mark in the Universe. Trial and error is just a way of life that helps us to learn better and easier ways to deal with stress, thus keeping our anger locked in the right box. Creating real and active possibilities is what we do in trying to find or create successful solutions for our future. At times we may go through miles and miles of "CRAAP" before we are able to find or see a solution. There are going to be days when your level of anger is going to be pushed beyond reasonable limits and "ME' asking myself, "ARE WE CURING CANCER IN THIS SITUATION," will seem like a true waste of your time. My main reason for asking myself this question is to allow myself a chance to slow down, take a deep breath, so I can bring the true details of the situation into FOCUS. Now you may not like using my question for one reason or another. You may decide to say "My life is worth more than a bad decision," or "Every day is mine and anger is not my ruler!" Whatever the phrase or question is, the point is to STOP, LOOK, and LISTEN. The "STOP" takes the immediate reaction out of the situation. It's the first step to keeping anger in the box. If anger doesn't have the opportunity to leave the box, you have an opportunity to maintain your FOCUS. After you stop, you need to always look. "LOOK" at everything going on around you. Look to keep everything in perspective by taking the emotion out of what you see. Learn to deal with each situation as just that. When I was a Deputy Sheriff on training, my Training Officer (Lee Edwards) would always tell me to handle each radio call to conclusion. You're finished with the call when all of your questions have been answered. Keep the human factor in front of what you see. After we look, we "LISTEN!" What are we listening too? We listen for where the root of anger is coming from. We listen to the voice we should trust giving us direction to be patient and listen to every word directed at you. Because I'm a Listener, I believe this is what gives me the patience I have today. The ability to listen has saved my life, literally on more than one occasion. Montel Williams has a quote that he often uses when he's speaking… "Speak without offending and listen without defending". Breaking this quote down to the bare facts, when you open your mouth to say something, remember you're speaking to another person! "A HUMAN BEING." Speak to them, even during a period of anger, with the same respect that you would like to hear something being said to you. If you can learn to stop, look and listen, I've found this quote will keep anger wrapped up in a tight little box, so you can move freely through your personal Matrix and find the success you're looking for. Anger can be a tool in your FOCUS arsenal if controlled properly. Peace, love and self-control, are the lights that shine in spite of anger and again, one can't exist without the other. Anger can become passion if pushed in the right direction. Your ability to control your anger is based on the work you put in. The question you chose to ask yourself "ARE WE CURING CANCER IN THIS SITUATION?" or whatever it may be is there to create that pause necessary to maintain control. Because we are creatures of habit, good and bad, we become most of our habits and those habits will ultimately create our environment.

After "ANGER" comes "DEPRESSION" and depression will come so you will have to also go through this too! You can survive it. Understanding FOCUS is one of the best ways to assist you in getting through this tough time. I have to thank God that FOCUS was developing in me… I didn't know it at the time, but in hindsight I understand its evolution. Depression is not only negative squared; I believe that it is, "EVIL ON EARTH!"

STEP TWO DEPRESSION:

Depression is a noun and is defined as:
1) A state of unhappiness and hopelessness
2) A psychiatric disorder showing symptoms such as persistent feelings of hopelessness, dejection, poor concentration, lack of energy, inability to sleep and sometimes-suicidal tendencies.

It's time to meditate again so look at the quote at the beginning of this chapter and read it again. Make it a part of your damaged Soul Step and let it get into your spirit because, depression is the deepest valley we have to travel through. Look at and meditate on the definition of depression for a few minutes. Take your time there is no rush because, we have a little work to do so we shouldn't rush through this. Depression is a noun and we know that nouns can be a person, place, or thing and I chose to make depression a thing! That gives depression substance and tangibility and for me that keeps it real. Making it real allows me the ability to deal with it and it's not just in my head, it's standing right in front of me. The power of our minds, are stronger than we could ever push them to be. Everyone has the ability to fight, you just need to find the right reason to stand up and do it. Why not for yourself?

LIFEWORK JOURNAL ENTRY

I wake up in the middle of the night and I lay in my bed staring into the darkness that is my room. In that darkness, is an emotion of anger not allowing me rest! Every Nano byte of anger in my bones comes to my mind and enters my Soul Step clouding my FOCUS. A clouded Soul Step will in many cases lead to depression and in this depressed state my Universe does not move. My Universe becomes a void as the deepest black hole in space, endless in its motion and without life. My environment is at an absolute stand still... nothing in, nothing out. During a period after my shoulder surgery where I flat lined, I went through a considerable amount of depression. Fortunately for me I rebounded quickly and was able to re-establish my FOCUS. There have been other times when I've been depressed and the fight to get back to level took a little more effort, but I was able to pull myself back.

END LIFEWORK JOURNAL ENTRY

To walk around every day feeling as though your life has no specific place in our Universe, is that feeling of hopelessness described in the definition of depression. I didn't realize how at the time depression had entered into and taken over my life to the degree it did. I stopped feeling the internal happiness that once gave my life purpose and everything I began to experience in the way of emotions, was cold and extremely bitter. I had never experienced this level of depression before in my life, ever! I can look back now and I said to myself at one point during this depression, "I didn't want to ever go through this shit again and I didn't!" Why does this hurt so badly and when will it end? These are just two of the endless questions I would ask myself every day. Each and every day I would sink lower and lower into the black hole that is depression. I remember asking myself, "Why are you so upset?" "Why are you allowing this feeling to have that much emotional control over your life and spirit?" Again, questions asked and I have no answers. I could barely get out of bed let alone answer a question of myself with any degree of clarity. If you've ever been in a very serious relationship and for one reason or another it didn't work out, this could create the type of depression, I was experiencing. If you've ever lost a family member or a close friend, this could cause that level of depression. We've all been there on some level, right? The truth in these situations although painful, is always better to know the truth. Finding out the truth in some cases is a blessing and a curse at the same time. No matter how you find out this so-called truth it is an eye-opening blessing. Eye opening because knowing is always the beginning to healing and understanding keeps you in a positive light allowing you to maintain your FOCUS. Eye opening because seeing clearly or with clarity is one of the only ways to move Focus Forward in your life. Notice I said "Your life," because that's exactly what it is… "YOUR LIFE!" The five clarities will be with you for the rest of your life now that you realize they exist. The darkness of depression and what it represents can cause you mental and physical pain and that mixed every other negative in your life could become the base of your depression. "You have to get up!"

LIFEWORK JOURNAL ENTRY

Here I am a Deputy Sheriff protecting the citizens of Los Angeles County and I'm depressed. I would rather stay in bed and hide under my covers than go to work, but off to work I go everyday doing my job to the best of my ability and my best was pretty damn good. As I look back at my life during that time I discovered I was able to hide my depression the same way I hid the "ANGER" chip that was embedded on my shoulder growing up. I also discovered there are so many people walking around every day depressed and they have learned just like I did to control it or "HIDE IT," go out and do their jobs just like everyone else. It's still there but I'm able to control it for extended periods of time every day. It's very sad but true! Something I have found, if you've ever been depressed or suffered from depression, I can look into someone's eyes and see they are battling with some sort of internal demon. That could also be because I am a "LISTENER," but I can see the depression like I'm watching a movie. What was once a happy existence, becomes a distant shadow of the life we once knew and that's because of our slow assimilation into this negative state. Sometimes the assimilation happens quickly because of a traumatic experience and once we are there, that black hole sucks us in like a tornado ripping up and destroying everything in its path. "You have to get up!"

END LIFEWORK JOURNAL ENTRY

The near-death experience that triggered my black hole of depression turned out to be more than just life changing. In this instance it made me stop, look and listen more, but it also gave me an amazing appreciation for the life that was given back to me. It truly gave me the ability to see beyond the exterior of everyone I've met and it connected me immediately to his or her spirit. If depression is pain, then pain must become a tool used for learning. Learning what to do when the pain of depression erupts is key in learning to fight depression. If you've ever experienced any bit of depression, then you know it's a fight you never give up on. No surrender, no retreat! This should be your mind set every day you open your eyes and every night before you go to sleep. One way to use pain to help you fight depression is to remember the feeling it's causing due to the pain. Clarity in memory, as humans we're in the habit of repeating those things that bring us the greatest amount of pleasure. It's human nature and it's in the make-up of our DNA. I don't know anyone who finds any pleasure in depression, but we get so used to accepting depression on so many levels and accept it as fact for our lives. Remember the assimilation to depression can be a slow process, almost natural in its scope even though it's negative in nature. We build up an incredible tolerance to the pain, causing us to lose sight of the main reason we are depressed. Many times, we have no idea that depression has become a driving force in our lives. We don't forget the true trigger of our original depression but once the trigger is set, we allow smaller triggers, to constantly push that button keeping us depressed. The next thing you know you are in so deep, so often, it has become home.

My original trigger of all the anger that grew in my spirit, (BELIEVING MY MOTHER DIDN'T WANT OR LOVE ME) discussed in the anger portion of this chapter from my experience with depression, I've found once you have that major trigger, it can put you in a depressed state of mind, over and over again! If allowed, everyday circumstances can create triggers keeping you in that black hole of depression. I didn't truly understand what was happening to me during this time or why the severity of my depression was so extreme. One day I decided to take a hard look at my depression and I started to study it like I was doing my own research study… and guess what? I came to a better understanding of my depression and I also realized if I could control it long enough to go to work and function at a high level, then there was hope I was not a lost cause. I also found because of FOCUS I managed to do some amazing things in my life thus far, depressed or not. One of the main things I realized is depression was not good for me, or the people close to me, especially my son Jammal. So, I thought to myself, "What can I do or what should I do to shake this pain and anger in my heart?"

First things first, "GET HELP!" A really good friend, who happens to be a psychologist, told me I needed to accept the fact that I'm depressed. That was not hard to do because I was truly depressed. I was also told by this same person to look at my life (which I did quite often) and look at the things that made me happy in the past. At the time I was in this black hole and I was not able to think any happy thoughts, "Are you crazy!" I asked her and she looked me right in the eye and said, "Is what you're doing working?" I thought about what she said over the next couple of weeks and as each hour of each day passed, even in my negative state flashes of happy thoughts entered into my consciousness through my subconscious from the files of my CIM. Because nothing happens overnight I find myself in a daily struggle between what I call good and evil. The age-old battle that will always be our lives. Used as nouns, "Good" and "Evil" fall under the category of things and because they do this gives them the necessary substance making them real for me. Even in my sad and depressed state I'm moving forward in my life and as I make this move I can see this very dim light deep in my eyes. Even though the light is dim the remarkable thing on the positive side of it is, there is light. I look in the mirror at the dim light in my eyes and as I do, I learn to FOCUS on that flicker of light and I feel the warmth in my heart beginning to ignite my Soul Step again. "I HAVE TO FULLY BELIEVE THIS!" I've found when you are depressed your heart becomes a very dark and cold box living inside you. I find it truly amazing how we can have this muscle in the center of our chest, the strongest muscle we possess pumping the life force of blood throughout our bodies and it can grow cold and feel empty. The dim light in my eyes can be the spark needed to allow my Soul Step to re-ignite. You need to search for and find that line between depression and forgiveness and learn to forgive yourself. Forgiving myself was a key factor in managing depression. That's where you have to start after you accept the fact you are depressed. In many cases we tend to blame ourselves for what triggered our depression in the first place. Learning to forgive oneself is difficult because of our make up as humans and because those triggers have the ability to take our depression deeper than ever. Working through the emotional, psychological and physical changes can continue to affect your world for years to come. There were times when I felt it was easier to just stay depressed. As you look back over your life and evaluate some of the triggers that caused your initial depression, this could be a great way to help you push through to that state of Enlightenment. The triggers that create your depression must be avoided at all cost, by continuing to learn every day and seek out what makes you happy. Every small setback when

I was trying to meet certain goals was a trigger for me! If the avoidable triggers are people, places or certain things then you need to let them go. Free will is always going to be your best friend so you can never, ever give up the fight for your life! A better quality of life for you and your family is always worth fighting for. No surrender, no retreat because depression will always do it's best to hold on and smash your world right where you live. Depression will try and squeeze the positive light right out of you and every dream you've ever had. I know because I lived through it! Being of strong mind and body I decided I would not let depression rule or control my life ever again. Hear me when I say depression is going to pack its bags of negativity and run out of my front door. It's not that simple, but the more you fight the stronger you will become and in time your strength will prevail giving you the upper hand over depression. Learning the power of FOCUS is the strength I was able to pull from during the times when my depression was at its worse. As I look back opportunities continued to present themselves to me and FOCUS allowed me to see that. You have to be strong enough when the walls are closing in around you, to use the keys you have to open the door and let yourself out. Making mistakes is not the end of the world and it's not the end of your world when it happens. Every mistake is just another challenge that has to be met. Mistakes being challenges, I would hope we are not challenged every moment of every day, but as mistakes go, so could you. Because the learning process is placed before you through hard work, your personal growth is what happens. You would never learn anything if you didn't make any mistakes. I'm not saying to go out and purposely create or make mistakes, but you need to accept that you will make them and surviving mistakes is not impossible. As I think about anger and how strong of a force it can be, if you don't learn to control it, it could consume you.

I know what you're thinking... how do I control depression? How do I control something that has such a strong hold on my life? Well first I would say if you have a chemical imbalance then you should seek the help of your doctor, a psychologist or a psychiatrist who is well equipped to help you through this challenging time. I would also say the same thing if your depression is so overwhelming and the duration of it truly becomes your life. Again, seek the help of a medical professional. Seeking help in any area, especially depression doesn't mean you're weak, gave in or gave up. Asking for help in real times of need is a true sign of strength. Having said that this is another way I've learned to control my depression. When I say control it, I've been able to control the duration and the severity of my depression. By looking at the "TRIGGERS" causing my depression, once I discover what those triggers are, that is the first step to building strength. One of the biggest keys to controlling my depression is "WORKING OUT!" Weight training and boxing have been a blessing and a Godsend for me. Physical activity has always been a source of strength for me: physically, mentally, spiritually, and emotionally. The other reward from training is the boost it gives your Soul Step through the "ENDORPHINS," (Endorphins interact with opiate receptors in the brain to reduce our perception of pain and act similarly to drugs such as morphine and codeine) it releases. Some of you may need professional help defining your triggers and again that's ok. Get help any way you can, so you can get back to living a productive life and continue moving Focus Forward.

LIFEWORK JOURNAL ENTRY

I have an extremely hard time with people I believe are being rude. Here I am coming from Southern California, where everyone speaks and a morning head nod to those you pass is commonplace. Now I'm two-thousand, seven-hundred and eighty-nine points four miles away in New York. Living in Manhattan where no one speaks and there is zero eye contact. When people pass you on the crowded sidewalk, you might get a hip check without an excuse me, before you get a good morning or a how do you do! You talk about pushing buttons… TRIGGERS!!! I bit my tongue so many times you would have thought I had it pierced. Clarity in Others taught me to take a step back and learn the ways of this new land. I told you before that New York has two speeds fast and faster. The people living here are some of the best people on the planet, but it took some getting used to. New York truly taught me, not to judge any book by its cover and you should at least read the foreword before you decide to throw it away. Sometimes you have to read the entire book and it could take time and patience. A "New Yorkers" disposition is not that they're rude, but New Yorkers are all about getting things done in what they call a "New York Minute!" In the rest of the world a "New York Minute" is about fifty seconds. No one really knows but it's fast. In this hindsight moment learning to accept and adapt to situations goes a long way in dealing with an ever-changing world and reducing stressful "TRIGGERS."

END LIFEWORK JOURNAL ENTRY

As you get older you will find people and situations that will be able to push your buttons so to speak sending you into crazy land. The people, you can choose to stay away from them for the most part avoiding that trigger. With other situations it has to be a step-by-step process and you must pay attention to the situation, almost dissecting every aspect of it looking for the clarity in it. Remember what I said about you choosing how you react or respond to things when they happen? You choose what happens when that one little thing goes wrong, or when things don't happen the way you had planned them. It could be something as little as getting phone calls too early in the morning or having an accident while you're on your way to work in the morning. Sometimes the smallest thing happening to you first thing in the morning, could be the first trigger in your day sending you into a black hole of depression by the end of your day. Depression took over my life once for what seemed like an eternity and getting out of it felt like I could never win. Remember "What Is Necessary" (WIN) is for you to fight! First thing in the morning is where the "WINNING" begins. I like to wake up at least 10 to 15 minutes before I have to look into the mirror and take my time with my life. No rushing around the room all flustered driving myself crazy, killing my FOCUS first thing in the morning. I try and make it a point to keep my stress level to a minimum. How I do that is to deal with and try to handle each little situation or challenge before they have the opportunity to grow and develop into something larger. If I have a situation (not a problem) with someone I work with, I address it with that person before it magnifies into something that can't be managed. It's the same thing at home or in my personal life. If there is a situation with your wife or husband, your girlfriend or boyfriend, or even with your parents or your children, address it with that person. Put all your cards on the table and deal with the situation. First, it will allow you tell someone how you feel, that way they can never say they didn't know you felt that way. Second, when you tell someone what's going on with you and how you're feeling it takes the pressure off of you and your Soul Step is not compromised. Remember you never know what someone is going through. Third, I like and respect when I know where I stand with people and that's one of the best ways to keep the pressure off. When people learn what your mindset is, it also makes them more comfortable. Stress can cause your mind and your body to go through so many changes sending your emotions into a tailspin that you may not be able to pull out of. Please don't let this happen to you! Remember if you try and learn to control how you react to things it not only takes the pressure off of you, but it makes little stresses much easier to deal with keeping those damn triggers under control. Anything worth working for is always worth fighting for! You have to believe you are worth everything you do. The longer you're in this depressed state the longer it will be before you accomplish the goals you have set for yourself. Depression clouds FOCUS and a clouded FOCUS will not allow you to see or understand "BOTAAE." Fighting through the monster "DEPRESSION" every day without failure is tough, but if you persist you will become better at it and the fight will become easier to manage. Perfect practice creates the success necessary to accomplish your goals. One day you will be able to push past this monster and grow to a level of Enlightenment allowing you to fulfill every dream, wish and desire that is truly in your heart. I'll say this once again NEVER GIVE UP!!!

STEP THREE ENLIGHTENMENT:

Enlightenment is a noun and is defined as…
1) The enlightenment of somebody or a cause of the enlightenment of somebody
2) A state attained when the cycle of reincarnation ends and desire and suffering are transcended or the achievement of this state.

If you could see my face right now you would see a smile so big and bright the North Star fails in comparison. The Anger and Depression portions of this chapter as painful as they were to write are extremely necessary in the development of your FOCUS. "WELCOME TO ENLIGHTENMENT!" It's time to free your mind, allowing it to expand to the Positive. The entire Universe is now at your command! Positive is a place I have grown to love and live in and I don't want to ever go back to "N" City. One of my favorite songs of all time was written in 1979 by McFadden & Whitehead, "AIN'T NO STOPPIN' US NOW" and it became one of my anthems, helping me through some really tough times. The lyrics are extremely uplifting, positive and they gave me a spirit of believing I could do anything. I gave birth to "ENLIGHTENMENT" and I didn't even know it…

Now I know what it means to W.I.N! Hard work is what we do to get to where we know we belong. Whatever you believe your life could or should be, is always up to you. Enlightenment is truly one of my favorite words and I have learned to live in it every day. I like this word because "YOU" have to come to the understanding about "YOUR" life and the situations that surround "YOU" that create "YOUR" Unlikely Destiny. As you grow to understand these situations, an ongoing level of growth and development can be achieved. When you become enlightened several pretty amazing things happen to you. Coming to your own understanding of things in your own time is a feeling that can only be described as simply amazing! It's kind of that feeling or the sensation that you get when you learn a complex math problem for the first time. As I child I remember the first time Geometry clicked in my brain and all I could do was smile! Excitement and discovery are truly amazing especially when they are yours. The feeling of Enlightenment as good as it feels can be somewhat overwhelming, but what a great feeling! Something else happens when you become enlightened: you learn "Forgiveness." As your spirit elevates, you will realize everything takes time and, in that time, you will discover forgiveness. I said this before about forgiveness and forgiving yourself is a tough fight, but it's a fight that can be won. When I look at the definition of Enlightenment there are several words in the two definitions that are key in your FOCUS. The word "Reincarnation" leaps off the pages of the dictionary at me. Reincarnation is a word that has a feeling or an air of mystery, but reincarnation in simple terms, is a reappearance of something in a new form. The key word here is, "New." When you reach a state of Enlightenment in your life, the way you look at yourself and everything around you will change (BOTAAE). Your approach to life will allow you to see with "ENLIGHTENED CLARITY." You will become one with, or open to your new environment. The Enlightenment is all about believing in and accepting opportunities meant for you that were earlier clouded by your "ANGER" and "DEPRESSION." How will your world change or become different? That's completely up to you, but if you allow the change to happen, the transformation or reincarnation you undergo will be life changing! Your senses will start absorbing everything out of thin air kind of like a magician pulling playing cards from behind your ears or pulling a rabbit out of a hat. You will become a new person in a manner of speaking and you will also begin to live your life with a true sense of purpose. Knowing why you are here gives you an advantage to living a better life and you will learn to move your life in a better direction or your direction of purpose. The light you saw shinning at the end of the tunnel is the light that will eventually surround you. Allowing yourself to shine is the true light guiding you in a new direction so, "FLOW WITH IT." Don't ever shrink your life or your dreams to make those around you feel more comfortable. The new confidence that develops in you is having a better understanding of yourself, but more importantly it is giving you a better attitude about your life. Understanding yourself creates a forgiving spirit and something new will always be allowed to happen for you, as well as others. This is pay dirt! Forgive! Forgive! Forgive! Learning the principles of forgiveness, gives you the ability to rebound faster from situations that could jeopardize your Enlightenment and your ability to FOCUS. You will be able to see how everything you experience, becomes a part of your environment and you will also learn to use every experience to your advantage. If you dwell on negative situations they could stunt your growth. The black hole that once pulled you into the depths of what is your own personal "HELL" won't have that same control over your life, like it did in the past. Trust me when I say skimming the surface of depression is a lot easier to recover from than being pulled into the endlessness of the black hole, where depression will attempt to take you. Knowing and understanding how Enlightenment has worked in my life became my saving grace. Being aware of my purpose and reason for being in the Universe, keeps me on track for greatness. Every morning I wake up I get out of bed and I say a silent prayer. I thank the Lord for allowing me to live another day and in this day, I will do something positive. That is my first daily affirmation. Then I make my way to the bathroom mirror where I stand working on and increasing my daily FOCUS. I'm always going to try and look deeper and deeper into myself so I can stay Focus Forward. One of the things I discovered about Enlightenment is as I look in the mirror I can see the world is ever changing and even though these changes take place on a daily basis, you can adapt. Being able to adapt to my life's changes comes from me wanting to change. From Opportunity Comes Unlimited Success and the best way to achieve that success, is to allow yourself to grow. It's yours to accept on so many levels and I know you're going to say; here he goes again with that "Free Will" stuff. Free will is the best part about Enlightenment because it already belongs to you. Enlightenment gives me an inner strength to win through will, as it manifests into something tangible. When you know the true meaning of words, they give you a different level of mental power. You can be any and everything you believe yourself to be, or talk yourself into. You "WILL" always be the strength in the change you need to make. Words have the meaning and power we give them so, give power to the right words and learn to live on the positive side of these words and grow accordingly. We are and will become what we believe…

LIFE WORK JOURNAL ENTRY

I remember working in the Los Angeles County Jail and I'd see several inmates reading the Webster Dictionary. They were looking at and trying to memorize words. At the time being the super intellectual Deputy Sheriff I was, I thought these inmates were morons. They had a lot of time on their hands, so to read the dictionary was a little ridiculous to me, but as time passed I found I was the ridiculous moron. As I thought a little more about it I said to myself knowledge is one of the best ways to free your mind. Being locked in a jail cell for an extended period of time everyday can become mentally and physically numbing to say the least, so I decided to open the dictionary myself and it's amazing what I discovered. I discovered even though I wasn't in jail, I was locked up with these inmates from 8 to 16 hours a day. My mind became incarcerated several hours a day for nearly two years. That's a lot of time when you think about it. So, don't knock it until you've tried it, or read it! It was during this time that I discovered my favorite word, "ENLIGHTENMENT." Learning how words influence our lives I've found you shouldn't give certain words any power. The "N" word can't be allowed to survive in your new world. In the strength that is your Enlightenment you should be able to find life-saving power in everything you do. If you want words to be life changing, then you will have to choose your words wisely and please learn what they mean when you use them.

END LIFEWORK JOURNAL ENTRY

Enlightenment is not just a word to me, it's a point of my FOCUS that has been developed through trial and error in my life. As the overall picture of my life comes into FOCUS the picture is not completely clear but that's okay. You see if you continue to grow and evolve, your Enlightenment should continue to develop every day you live. The picture (YOUR LIFE) as beautiful as it may be should never be completed. The picture I've developed in my mind's eye is abstract in its content. I keep it abstract because, as parts and pieces of thoughts develop in my mind, they may not fit perfectly at that time, but keeping them abstract gives me the ability to make them fit, where I need them to fit. Change is constant… another perpetual motion of sorts. Because change is constant, as we adapt to our environment, our environment adapts to us, and our needs. The true term "EXPERT" should be attached to or followed by the phrase "ALWAYS LEARNING." Over the years I've stayed away from using the word "EXPERT" or wanting to call myself by that term. Because of my experience in law enforcement and personal security, people have tried to pin me an expert. Speaking of expert let's look at the definition…

Expert is a noun and it is defined as:
1) Somebody with a great deal of knowledge about or skill training or experience in a particular field or activity.

The definition of expert does not say an expert knows everything. Experts have knowledge in a particular field or an area of training, but they don't know everything. Doctors on any level, as much as people think or believe they do, don't know everything. God bless them for the knowledge they do have, but learning should always be a life long journey, especially for doctors. My true feeling is, as long as I live I will continue to learn. I just want you to always think for yourself and always, always do your homework! I don't want to ever become an "EXPERT" in the way our society looks at the word expert, or the person carrying the title. As I continue to learn that allows my Enlightenment to remain ever increasing. So, the next time someone calls you an expert you need to take a step back and tell them you are a, "CHILD OF ENLIGHTMENT" and your quest for knowledge is never ending. This is what I believe has kept me and my clients satisfied with my work. My Soul Step in check keeps my skills always sharp and ready.

In Chapter One I asked you to "Free Your Mind" to get you thinking to understand your evolution to Enlightenment, so it won't come to you as a total shock. Learning to free your mind is essential in freethinking and opening yourself up to new and different things. Nothing happens in your life unless you make it, or allow it to happen. You make things happen by taking charge or control of your life, staying focused and putting your plans in action. Think about it… what happens when you do nothing? It's Your FOCUS, your plan and your life! Allowing things to happen without a plan, does not give you the control necessary to stay on the positive side of your life. No FOCUS, No Plan and most of all no control over the life you're living! The words living inside me, in my spirit, in my heart and now on these pages, would never have been discovered without understanding Enlightenment, but I had to also realized the words were put there for me to write. I spoke earlier about knowledge: Having it, knowing it and using the knowledge you've acquired to make your life and the lives of the people close to you better. Better in the sense that, when you know something about yourself or your circumstance, with knowledge you can make the necessary changes to develop a better life. So many times, we continue to live our lives according to an old circumstance, or the cards we were dealt. Even when we learn new things we continue to allow the "N" word to dominate our everyday existence. As they say "Old habits are hard to break" and that would be true, if you were not developing a better attitude and outlook. Hard maybe, but not impossible to break! What you need to do is reshuffle the deck of cards you hold and deal yourself a new hand. With the knowledge you've acquired, and the new cards you hold you can now show your cards face up, allowing your success to shine. You can also look at the cards you now hold, the same as the keys you are learning to use to open doors. You have to put the key in the lock, turn it, open the door and walk inside. Once inside you have to be ready for what you encounter. The circumstances you once lived your life under may still exist, but you no longer have to react in a negative way to that circumstance. The way you respond to situations or possible setbacks will no longer have to consume your existence. Learning to deal with situations and how you allow every situation to affect you, is key in your recovery from them. FOCUS is like going into to rehab… "I say Yes, Yes, Yes." After you leave therapy you learn techniques that help you and give you the ability to deal with your world. When you close this book and have to go out and deal with things in your daily life, I hope Unlikely Destiny gives you some positive tools allowing you to move Focus Forward. I hope it helps you see beyond the Matrix. Live your life, don't let your life live you. Every day you wake up, the circumstance you may be living at the moment should not be your final resting place, or will it? That's completely up to you. You're going to have to stop the cycle of negative that creates a particular circumstance and get back to living again. When I look back over my life and I sift through situations that caused my anger and depression, I realize I missed so many opportunities, because my FOCUS was clouded for an extended period of time. Clarity in Memory, allows me to see these situations, and in my review, I find myself a little taken back because at the times, I didn't understand how to deal with certain issues, that lead to my stress. Stress will and can only win if you don't deal with it. If you don't step up and meet stress or anything in your life head on, you allow it to win. Throughout my years in Law Enforcement and Private Security I found that stress is not only a part of my daily routine it's expected. When you are charged to protect a city, or someone's life, there is a certain level of stress involved in this process. Because of Enlightenment I have learned to feed off of the stress I feel when I'm working. I use the stress to keep me sharp and conscious of my surroundings. The positive side of stress keeps me extremely focused. Another way of handling your stress is always doing your homework! Get the information you need, so when things change in your daily circumstance you are prepared and don't panic. The Unconscious Consciousness where I learned to live my life has come through Enlightenment. Because of Enlightenment I don't over think everything anymore. I look at the way things happen in our lives naturally and without over thinking, I have learned to adapt to situations. I look at it the same way you would, if you were driving a car. Once you learn how to drive a car you don't have to think about driving the car, but you do have to be aware of your driving, the other driver's around you and the streets you are traveling on. That is your Unconscious Consciousness at work. I don't have to think about being positive anymore because positive is where I live my life. Enlightenment evolves freely from within and like I said it's not given to you by anyone, it's yours to accept as a natural part of your life. Take control of your life and live it the way it is meant to be, with success! Success is measured on so many levels and the best part of this equation is you! You determine the amount of effort you want to give to your life and your purpose. The final outcome of your effort should be success!

As you move forward through your Anger and Depression evolving into your Enlightenment the other side of this is, "CLARITY." I want you to use the Five Clarities, because they will help you to maintain your FOCUS, keeping you at that constant stage of Enlightenment. Because you have moved forward to an even more positive side of your life, it is beginning to align like the stars you see in the heavens. Where do we go from here? Look up… Now that your vision is clear, what do you see?

8

Now That Your Vision Is Clear,
What Do You See?

The most satisfying thing in life is to have been able to give a large part of one's self to others…

Pierre Teihard de Chardin

I've opened my mind, my heart and my spirit and with my Soul Step Focus Forward, I can see everything before me. My eyes are open and my vision is clear, guess what I see? **EVERYTHING!** Let's start this chapter by having another look at the words Vision and Clear:

Vision is a pronoun and it is defined as*:
1) The ability to see.
2) An image or concept in the imagination.
3) An image or series of images seen in a dream or trance often interrupted as having religious revelatory or prophetic significance.

Clear is an adjective and it is defined as:
1) Free from anything that darkens or obscures.
2) Able to be seen through.
3) Easily heard or seen
4) Easy to understand and without ambiguity.

As I look at the definition for each of these words, with vision, it is clear, I am evolving. You could say, "I've grown to Enlightenment!" I could also say I am growing up in so many ways. Even as I am writing Unlikely Destiny my vision is clearer than when I started this process. There is a vision or idea, we all have of ourselves and in most cases this vision is not clear to us at all. Most of the time we don't see what we are supposed to see and since we don't see clearly, we miss many of the things that are placed before us, that are for us. A major part of vision or being able to see clearly is understanding an opportunity when it's presented to you. In many cases we still see what we believe. It's that flawed individual in the mirror looking back at us. We still see the circumstance we grew up with, even during times when we find our greatest success, we feel our worth is not in line with the hard work we've put in. Often times our feelings tell us, we don't have any worth in this Universe. This is where that feeling or opinion of yourself has to stop! Our lives are filled with so many opportunities, we often lose out on them because we don't think they are for us. I know I keep saying this, but it's time for you to get it. How many times have you heard a story about the person who was asked by their best friend to go to an audition with them, or they are asked to do something else in a similar fashion and the person doing the asking loses out on the opportunity, because the friend gets the job? The person who winds up landing the job in these situations, did they take advantage of an opportunity or was this opportunity meant for this person? I used to wonder how the friend could do that to someone they consider a friend? That seemed like a very mean thing to do to someone you consider a friend. Before I came to understand Unlikely Destiny, that was my mindset, but I have since learned to look at life and opportunities a little differently. If you think about our Universe there are many things that we just don't understand and it's okay. The person who goes to that audition and they invite their best friend, you have to wonder to yourself why and how the invited person gets the job. I think this is something that will haunt all of us for many years to come, but I have an idea… I want you to think about what I have been telling you, since you opened this book… "Things happen in your life the way they are supposed to." Even in what we believe is a negative situation, I see the clarity on the other side of it. I have to believe you were put in the position to help the other person. This door may seem to have closed, but if you put away the "PSUEDO-ANGER" and learn to be genuinely happy at the success of others in this situation, bigger and better opportunities will be yours for the taking. You may not even understand why you asked this person to go with you that day and neither will they, but it's ok, our Universe is doing its job. Continue to look to where it is you want to go and begin moving your life in that direction. Look at what I just said "Begin moving your life in that direction." You have to learn to be fully committed to whatever it is you're doing. You invite your friend to the audition with you because your level of confidence (SOUL STEP) isn't what it should be. When your friend auditions they feel as though they have nothing to lose, but even though they feel this way, they commit, Focus Forward and walk out of the audition with success. The good thing about being committed is when you look to take a certain direction in your life, if you don't make a total commitment then why waste your time. Like they say in poker, "You have to be all in!"

Are you beginning to understand the 95% to 5% theory I have about life? Are you also learning how that little 5% effort can make a big difference in your life? The 5% effort you put into everything will help you to see things much clearer. I have a quote for you to meditate on, said by Tiger Woods, "I believe going into every match that I am going win!" When I heard Tiger say this he spoke in his calm and somewhat tranquil demeanor, but his eyes meant every word that he spoke. I'm going to say to you, if you are not of the mindset that you have the ability to accomplish your goals, you need to continue to re-evaluate the reflection you see in the mirror. What do you see? Tiger's competitive Soul Step is always Focus Forward and the Clarity In Vision he sees with gives him a competitive edge. I know that Tiger Woods is a person before he is an athlete and I also realize his father saw something in him at an early age and pointed him in the direction of golf. The FOCUS he uses in his approach to golf clearly shows he has his PDD moving in the right direction. As long as he continues to study his craft and trust the process and his abilities, he will always be a winner. You are stronger than you know and you have always had that strength, but you were just too afraid to see it, show it, use it, or believe in it! Or maybe you confused confidence with arrogance. This is why knowing what the words we use mean in our daily lives, is so important. We exist on this planet and in this Universe for most of our lives as individuals, but as we become adults we tend to sometimes lose our individuality. In many ways we conform to the negative world around us and give up on our dreams and sometimes we get lost in the environment we create. We lose sight of the abilities we are born with by stuffing them deep into our box. When you lose sight of these abilities this could keep you from putting in any effort, let alone the 5% necessary to be successful at anything. The beauty of knowing you have certain talents or abilities is the full knowledge that they exist.

LIFEWORK JOURNAL ENTRY

I have heard people say, "I was born alone and I will die alone," but I beg to differ with this, because we all had to have a mother, who is there when we are born (EVEN JESUS HAD A MOTHER). Now since she just happened to be there, what does that tell you? Come on think about that one for a minute or two. Okay put the book down and call your mother and thank her. Thank her for giving birth to you, but most of all thank her for taking care of and raising you, so you could grow up and become the individual you are today. You have to be thinking to yourself, "Yes I am special!" You are, or will become the light that shines every day for someone other than yourself. Keep that in mind the next time you begin to lose FOCUS. The opportunities that are shared with you are not only for you they are for everyone you bring into your environment. Being an individual is important and once you realize how important you are, your inner strength will begin to show you when to be a part of a team. Even as we live with our family and friends we are still individuals and that's okay. Being an individual is what makes you who you are. The individual is whom people see when they meet you and that is a true blessing. As individuals we are often judged by the jobs we do, or sometimes for the circumstances surrounding our lives. We are also judged by the color of our skin, the people we know and the "GOD" we believe in and serve. I feel being judged this way, many times causes the people judging you, to lose sight of the true person standing before them (CLARITY IN OTHERS). Don't let what you see or the preconceived idea you have about someone destroy an opportunity that has been placed before you. Remember we are all going to need "HELP" at some point on our journey…

END LIFEWORK JOURNAL ENTRY

All I ask is that you learn to open your eyes and see the entire world you live in and the Universe you are a part of. A job title or a life circumstance does not define the individual standing before you, but the actions in your life, as the individual, is what I have learned to see. How clear is your vision and what do you see? During the past twenty-five years of my life I have spent many, many years traveling the world. During this time, I have learned to see beyond the person cleaning my hotel room, or the man riding on the back of the truck picking up my garbage, or the security guard who watches over you, as you work in the office building you spend a majority of your life in. They are always individuals first! They have lives and ideas and in most cases a plan beyond what you see them doing. Take a minute and have a conversation with someone outside of what you consider your closed inner circle and prepare in some cases to be amazed! They are human beings who contribute to our shared Universe every day.

A person could tell you every day, morning, noon, and night they love you and it's one of the single most amazing things you can hear… but telling someone you love them is one thing. I need for you to show me you love me by your actions. And if you do that you never have to say another word. The point that I'm trying to make is, I don't think it's fair to judge people, or pigeon hole them only seeing the person for what they do for a living, or where they live, or for the clothes they may be able to afford, or what someone else in their family has done… I could do this all day. We are more than that and we have a lot more to give than the life you may see before you. In order to get a clearer picture of the individual, you need to be BOTAAE and destroy the narrow mind you are currently using. Remember your circumstance is not your life it is merely a place that exists right now, but this place should never be allowed to determine your fate by you or anyone else. The best way to keep your vision clear is for you to learn to see everything the way it's supposed to be. We are "HUMANS BEINGS" before anything and I believe often times the human element is left out of our vision. When a coin is flipped in the air it lands on either heads or tails, depending on which one you chose, it could be either good or not such a good situation. Keep in mind you don't have any control over which side the coin lands on, but you do have control over how you react, to the flip of the coin. What do you see? With the proper vision and clarity, you control you. You can be rational letting your Soul

Step flow and keep your composure, or you can fly off the handle and lose the control, that allows you to think respectfully of others and maintain your FOCUS. I keep saying you, you, you, but "YOU" are the bottom line in your life. You can be as strong as you allow yourself to be or you can wither and die giving in to the pressures of your life. It is always your choice. People give up every day and in giving up, I mean they lose sight or lose the vision of their dreams. Sometimes we need to take a step back and refocus, so we can see our vision clearly again. I have always said to my family and friends "If you don't see the vision don't you stop the dream!" I know what you're saying, what the hell does that mean? Well it's like this, "My vision is my vision." I see myself as a writer and because I see my vision this way, I live and breathe every day to create something with my mind, then I put pen to paper and I find success. I have found when you have something inside you that you must get out, most of the people in your life may not fully understand (YOUR VISION) and that's okay. You have to learn to let negativity go and continue to run your race. You may not understand someone else's motivation to do something, but all I can ask you to do, is just learn to be supportive and positive about their passion(s) and their vision. I've achieved and completed one of the first of many writing goals. I had an idea and now it's out of my head and on the pages of this book. That was my clear vision and at the same time some of my friends and family didn't understand or see my dreams, but they have learned, through a lot of hard work, to be supportive, because now they can see the physical manifestation of the vision that was in my spirit. They also know I'm going to do my homework in whatever it is I want to accomplish. Another reason my family and friends support me, is because they know the person I am and they don't only see "ME" as what I do for a living. In order to accomplish anything, I've made it a point to never give up! I'd have to say, I have encountered a couple of situations, even as I write this book, there are some people that know me and they can only see me as a former deputy sheriff, police officer, or somebody's bodyguard. Before I discovered Enlightenment the thought of someone putting me where they wanted me to be, would have pushed me over the edge, but since my FOCUS is strong I can't be pushed off my mark. Remember how I told you fear kept me from writing Unlikely Destiny… well most of it was fear, but part of it was the fact that I did not have a clear vision of this book several years before writing it. Those days are officially over! My vision is clear and because I understand human nature and how perception works, I've been able to do a complete 180. My mindset and my Soul Step are completely in check and I can see everything. (BOTAAE) What do you see?

I want you to think back to chapters 2 and 3... Look in the mirror and ask yourself, why are you here? Looking at these two chapters in the beginning of this book you may not have had a clue as to who you really are and you probably never thought about why you were here. The vision you had of yourself wasn't so clear so don't be surprised if you didn't have a clear vision of anything, when I asked you to look in the mirror. Think about it for a minute and if you are anything like me before Enlightenment I didn't have a clue either. As I began living life on the positive side, I began to look in the mirror with a larger sense of purpose. As I looked at why I was here, I began believing in why I was here... now that my vision is clear guess what I see? Everything! I began to truly believe in my abilities and myself! I began to believe... I see writer first, but I'm still a listener. Remember there are things that we have to do (LISTENER) and there are things that we want to do, that can also become something we must do (WRITER). If in your vision you don't see yourself somewhere in there giving back, then you're going to have to find the time to meditate on that because, it's something we all must do. Giving back is the best form of help in our Universe. I said this earlier about listening and how it may not seem important to the average person. I also told you I decided to stop listening and when I did people came out of the wood work to tell me their inner most thoughts, ideas, and feelings. When I realized my listening was what the Universe gave me to give back, I opened my ears, mind, heart and spirit and listened without any questions. When I look at my personal life, my law enforcement career and personal security career, giving back becomes a necessity of the job, thereby giving balance to my side of our Universe. The simple formula to all of this is learning to work smart, but hard. The harder you work at FOCUS the clearer your vision will become. There are going to be good days and not so good days, but anything worth having is truly worth working for! Something I don't ever want you to forget as long as you live about this life is, "IT'S NEVER TOO LATE!" Having a clear vision doesn't equal age. You can't be too young or too old to achieve success. Remember what FOCUS means... From Opportunity Comes

Unlimited Success and your success can come at any time or any age. The sooner you realize, at whatever age opportunities are meant for you, your success will always be within reach. I just want you to be ready and recognize the opportunity when success happens.

Now that you live with Enlightenment, nothing happens to you, or for you by accident anymore. Don't go yelling at the book about something I just said. I'm not saying accidents don't happen, I'm just trying to get you to look at them when they do and you have to ask yourself on the positive side… why did it happen? I want you to look at every situation, even the direst circumstance and learn to see the positive side of it. Even in moments when your vision is blurred look to FOCUS for clarity. There is always a reason everything happens, so again understand it, but stay on the positive side of what happens. As long as you're alive, live like it! Every situation is just that, a situation and every one of them can always be worked through. I guess because of where I grew up, even when I wasn't focused I couldn't understand the mindset of a person who did not live their life with a sense of purpose, or a willingness to succeed. As the vision you have becomes clear, know that you won't be able to do any of the things you want to do, without help and when you get that help be willing to accept it. When you give back especially to those who help you reach your goal, this is always the best way to keep balance in the Universe. When it comes to your vision and being clear in all that you see, if you don't believe in it, then how do you expect those around you to believe in it, or you? Your actions and convictions will keep your vision clear and when people ask you what do you see, you can always say "Everything!"

Here's another Matrix reference to stress a point: If you saw the first Matrix movie, during the film the Neo character kept hearing over and over that he was "THE ONE." Neo had serious doubts about being "THE ONE" in the beginning and wouldn't believe it to save his life. He didn't even know what "THE ONE" was at the time. Like I said before, nothing happens overnight. It wasn't until Neo was enlightened that he began to believe in his purpose. He not only believed in what he was told by Morpheus, but most importantly Neo began to believe in himself and that allowed others to believe him and his purpose. You can read Unlikely Destiny from cover to cover, but until you begin to apply the principals to your life and begin believing in yourself, your vision will remain clouded for years to come. Looking back at Neo it literally took him getting shot before he truly believed in himself enough to stand up to the Agents and fight back. Neo's reality is a little bit different. He's seeing the world in a new light. Because he could see beyond the Matrix, he is able to see the world in streams of numbers or the computers kinetic codes, which is his new vision's reality. He also has defeated his fear of the Agents and he attacked them head on, without fear of any consequence. As harsh as his new reality is, it has prepared him for any changes that may come his way. Neo eventually overcame his circumstance because he began to believe. You have to FOCUS in order to move FORWARD and learn to accept the POSITIVE things in front of you, but you have to realize you can make changes. Creating the right FOCUS will help you to overcome your present circumstance. If your present circumstance is not your life, (AND IT'S NOT) then that should leave plenty of room, to still dream. When I look at the definition of vision, the word "DREAM" appears in the third definition and it just popped off the page at me. Growing up where I grew up dreaming for me became second nature. In the circumstance that surrounded my life at the time, I often thought I would live like this for the rest of my life, but I never gave up hope. I thank God for FOCUS and my ability to see it. As I got older I discovered dreams were the best way for me to escape my circumstances by creating a new reality, to one day live a better life. Speaking of dreams let's look at the definition.

Dream is a noun and it is defined as:
1) A sequence of images that appear involuntary to the mind of a sleeping person often a mixture of real and imaginary characters, places and events.
2) A series of images, usually pleasant ones that pass through the mind of someone who is awake.
3) Something that somebody hopes, longs, or is ambitious for, usually something difficult to attain or far removed from present circumstances.

I gave you the first three definitions of "DREAM" because they are clear and truly complete my vision. I have to say I have been told several times in my life that dreaming is a waste of time and most of the time they don't take you anywhere. When I was younger I think I was too naïve to stop dreaming. As I look back from a focused state, even when I was told to stop dreaming, I remember only a few people saying "most of the time dreams don't take you anywhere." By using the word "MOST" these people even had a doubt in their negative response to my dreams. If that's not funny, I don't know what is. It only takes one "DREAM CRUSHER" to change the course of your life, if you allow it to happen. Look at the third definition of "DREAM" and that is the exact reason we dream: Something that somebody hopes, longs or is ambitious for, usually something difficult to attain or far from present circumstances. Again, I'm going to continue telling you, "Believe beyond what you are living and learn to see what is in your heart as your true reality and work at finding a way to bring that vision to life." People do it every day, why can't you? Why shouldn't you? Even though our dreams may be difficult to attain they are not impossible. Keep Dreaming! You have to start believing every dream you have is a gift for you and it was given to you for a good reason. Because you can do it! I will never give up dreaming and I hope you will continue to dream on, all day every day. Even when times weren't so great I continued to dream. Even though some people continued to tell me dreaming was a waste of time, I learned to dismiss their negativity and I never altered my vision. If I listened to any of these people I would not be writing this book and Unlikely Destiny would have been just big blur in my life, left stuffed in my box. As I look at the third definition of dream that seals the deal for me. It encompasses everything to keep dreams alive. In the second definition it speaks directly to dreaming while you're awake. If you remember in chapter two, the five clarities again come into FOCUS. Clarity in Vision speaks directly to dreaming while you are awake. Your unconscious consciousness creates a constant dream state allowing you to dream, by keeping your dreams in perspective, and that's one of the reasons I told you earlier to, "Get your life in line with your goals!" Clarity in Vision will allow your vision to become so clear, that your visions will almost appear to be real. So real they will almost seem like your dreams. Wow, dreaming while you're awake… tell me what you see? A little clearer I hope. Picture this… everything you've always wanted to do getting done! Picture a world where working on ideas that have been buried in your heart or your spirit forever, now completed. Picture a world where you have the ability to see the world and I mean truly see the world you live in. Wouldn't it be amazing? Let me answer that for you, "YES IT WOULD!" Consider your life and everything you've been through. If you can look at your life and see any room for improvement, then consider your options. You can continue to live your life without even the thought of a dream, without imagination, no thoughts of doing anything, or you can learn to change your mind. You can look to that place in the back of your mind and spirit and let the dreams flow again. Why do you think you still have them? Let your imagination help to shape your future and accept the positive change your life has undertaken and stop fighting your success! Everything you do from this day forward, every decision, every idea, every vision, every moment of clarity is yours for the taking. Take a minute and meditate on that. It's okay just let it flow. Well look at that… your Soul Step is being fueled to take over, but only if you allow yourself to be positive and live that same way.

Another option in dreaming is when should you push and when should you pull? This is extremely necessary in dealing with family, friends, co-workers and just about anyone you meet. Give and take is another way to say push and pull. As a listener I have found that sometimes people just need to know you're there and other times they need your full input and participation. You have to look at each situation and evaluate accordingly. Keep in mind when someone finds a solution to their own situation, it gives them a feeling of accomplishment, so learn to always listen first. There are times in your life when your vision will be as clear, as some days are long. And then there will be days when your vision is clouded and you're going to have to understand, that there is a balance in life and somewhere in the middle of that balance is "YOU." For years I have looked at the Yin and Yang Symbol of balance in Chinese philosophy. I like what it represents and for me how it helps to keep balance in my life. Remember I am what society would call a Gemini according to astrology, the twins. They say Gemini's are always torn between the two sides, but I say the twins are a symbol of balance that occurs naturally in the Universe. The Yin and Yang symbol is also used in Korean philosophy and again they both use it in their description of balance. That balance refers to how seemingly opposing forces are bound together, intertwined and independent in the natural world, giving rise to each in turn. This symbol also lies at the heart of many branches of classical Chinese science and philosophy as well as being a primary guideline of traditional Chinese medicine. The relationship between Yin and Yang is often described in terms of sunlight playing over a mountain and in the valley. Yin (literally the "shady place" or the "North Slope") is the dark area occluded by the mountain's bulk, while Yang (Literally the "sunny place" or the "South Slope") is the brightly lit portion. As the sun moves across the sky Yin and Yang gradually trade places with each other, revealing what was obscured and obscuring what was revealed Yin usually characterized as slow, soft, insubstantial, diffuse, cold, wet and tranquil. It is generally associated with the feminine birth and generation and with the night. Yang by contrast is characterized as hard, fast, solid, dry, focused, hot, and aggressive. It is associated with masculine and daytime.

I gave you this information about the Yin and the Yang, because I want you to understand that there are two sides to everything. There is a positive and a negative, strength and weakness, day and night, and don't let me forget the truth and a lie. I could go on for days looking at both sides of every equation, but I'm not going to put you through that. What I will do is ask you to look within and find the balance that is inside you, created when you know it exists, remembering what I said about knowledge, so learn to use it. The Yin and Yang we have within ourselves meet at a midpoint with one another, allowing us to borrow from each side when necessary, in order to keep balance. The vision you have formed and maintained in your spirit all of your life is ready to be unleashed, the same way I unleashed Unlikely Destiny from my spirit onto the pages of this book. I had the vision to write Unlikely Destiny, but I was not clear in my thoughts to carry out the task. Being able to finally write this book has been a blessing to me. My wish is to pass on this feeling of joy inside my heart, now that my vision is clear. I believe this is one of the main reasons for me writing Unlikely Destiny. I want everyone reading the words on these pages to understand that they can feel joy, happiness, strength, the power to change, forgiveness, but most of all I want everyone to feel the same sense of Enlightenment that fills my heart every day. Look deep inside yourself… I will ask you again; Now that your vision is clear what do you see? Need I say everything? This is going seem a little like I'm contradicting myself, but there will be times in your life that you will have to be positive and negative, there will also be times in your life that you will have to show strength and other times you will have to let weakness be your guide. After each day, night must fall and that cycle has occurred one after the other, from the dawn of man. You should make it a point and try never to lie, but I will tell you that there will be times in your life if you do decide to tell the truth, in a particular situation that could be one of the worst mistakes you could ever make. Learning when to do what, is a part of the balance that you will have to decide, when and how you need to use it. Learn to listen to the voice of reason inside.

In the information I gave you about the Yin and Yang I like the word "FOCUSED" in the explanation of Yang. If you stop and look at your life, let me tell you that FOCUS is all around you. With the knowledge you have about FOCUS now, it can't be ignored. It's yours so take it and keep it moving. I'm going to ask you again… what do you see? You should see, a multitude of new beginnings. You should see success in your life where there use to be failure. You should see, hope in your future and the future of everyone you meet. When you look in the mirror, you should see, a never-ending future and success at every turn. Every day is a new day and as clear as that day is, you are strong, you are focused and directed in all that you do. Let's look again at your life and let's say you've never had a clear vision of anything… EVER! You have ambition to do something, but you just can't put your finger on it. That's when you need to go back and look at your Pros and Cons list. If you look at this list and study it, just a little I'm sure you will find something triggers your Soul Step and then, you need to act on it and don't look back. Your success could be one positive action away. I feel that one of the keys to bring your vision into clear FOCUS is through hard work. Think about it… how does a great athlete become great? Mastery is always earned through extreme effort! Nothing less will ever be accepted. The balance I spoke of earlier is extremely necessary because it will keep you grounded enough to help you work through your visions' quest. The Universe is your sandbox, but remember "YOU" have to share the sandbox with others. This is also where give and take plays an important role in your life. We all have to take from time to time. It's kind of like driving a car forward, but every so often we have to go in reverse. This is the give; still necessary to get where you have to go. In the natural order of life, I believe all giving must be from the heart, with an open hand. Remember what I said about the fist (NOTHING IN OR OUT). The fist is pretty much only good for punching. If someone falls down, the gesture is always an open hand to help them up, not a fist. Everyone needs a hand from time to time, and no one is beneath it, or above it! The main point that I'm trying to make in this chapter is your vision should include more than just you. Your idea is yours and you came up with it all on your own. You build a prototype for the greatest invention of all time, but you still need help to build it, promote it and create the brand to carry the success. You will need patent attorneys, consultants, researchers and who knows what else. As time moves forward and your life leans toward the positive, you have to understand everybody that needs help, and that help could be partly your duty to administer. Even as I write this book I'm going to need a whole boatload of help. Even if I self-publish, "UNLIKELY DESTINY VOLUME ONE," I'm going to have to depend on other people with every aspect of it. You can and need to work hard on everything you do, but hard work goes out the window if it's not shared. Dream a dream of success and always be proud in that success. Always work hard and your hard work will be a footprint for you and others for years to come. We live in a world where everything matters and everything you do counts. You will continue to grow as a person and as you grow, your faith in yourself and the people you bring into your environment, will begin to develop to a higher level. As you grow, you will learn whom to trust and that trust will help you continue to work on your abstract painting. Again, never completed, always a work in progress. In the development of your faith always remember to keep an open heart. Your development in this book is moving at a steady pace Focus Forward. I truly hope you are ready to win because there are, "No More Excuses… You Can Win."

No More Excuses… "You Can Win"

A thing of beauty is a joy forever

John Keats

John Keats was an English poet, born in 1795 and died in 1821. He was considered one of the greatest English poets of his time. I picked Keats' quote, "A thing of beauty is a joy forever", because coming out of Chapter 8; I wanted to ask you again, WHAT DO YOU SEE? I see a person, who will no longer look to make any excuses to fail in life. I see a person who has learned to do what is necessary to achieve their goals. I see a person who now believes they have a point and purpose in life, but most of all I want you to see that living your dreams is not only possible, it should be your Unlikely Destiny and the beauty you seek. This is truly A THING OF BEAUTY, when you come to an understanding, through Enlightenment that you can WIN. This "IS A JOY FOREVER!"

For the beauty that is you, should always come from within. You have to learn, what matters most with you and everyone you meet, is what's inside. Internally is where our true beauty originates and that internal beauty is what helps to balance the positive side of our Environment and our Universe. This allows you to be yourself and it also allows you to make everyone in your environment better. Creating an environment full of positive, focused and motivated people is bound to equal success on every level. The true beauty inside each of us, is what we were put here to do. Whatever has been placed in your spirit to do, enhances your beauty. Think about it… if you are doing what you love to do, especially for a living, even when times are difficult it still doesn't feel like work. The happier you are in your everyday life, at work and at home, this becomes the great equalizer with you and the Universe. Increasing your Soul Step is the next phase for you and your ability to W.I.N. When you learn how to win, because "WINNING" just like losing, is a learned behavior, you will discover unless you work at the development of your Unconscious Consciousness, your soul step will remain in a dormant state. As your heart beats with every step you take, success can always be within reach. Every day you wake up this gives you another opportunity to succeed. The outer you will begin to grow and shine, as bright as a full moon. Talk about finding your way home. Home is truly where the heart is and its where your spirit flows. Now take a minute and to shut your brain down for a few and allow your spirit speak for itself. Your spirit is where everything that is you originates. It is the core of your DNA. Deep within the spirit of each and every one of us, is the person you aspire to become. It's time to come home. PDD is straight from the spirit and this is where 95% of everything inside us comes from. The phrase, "He or she is high spirited," (FULL OF ENERGY AND HAPPINESS) has significant meaning when you know what it truly means. If PDD is the core of your existence, what are you passionate about and are you moving in that direction? Remember the 5% effort is what you decide to make it, moving you to the next level of completing every task before you. I heard the most amazing quote the other day and I'm sure it's been said before, but Hip Hop / R&B Artist, Trey Songz said… "HARD WORK BEATS TALENT, IF TALENT DOESN'T WORK HARD!" I can't get this quote out of my head. Your PDD what drives your God given abilities, but if it is not cultivated, nurtured, or allowed to grow, your abilities will never develop causing them to be wasted and taking your spirit to zero. No more excuses you can win, it's just that simple. You can win, but you have to work! Nothing can stop you from doing anything except you. You can take everything you've learned and do what is necessary to meet and accomplish every goal. Since I'm the king of the acronyms, of course I had to create one for the word "WIN." You actually read it earlier in this book and in this paragraph. "WHAT IS NECESSARY" equals "WIN" in my book every day! You hear the phrase "What is Necessary" time and time again and you probably never equated it to mean, win. Any and every one who has said, "WHAT IS NECESSARY" is ready to do any and everything to complete the task at hand. Let's look at the definition of the word win.

Win is a verb and it is described as:
1) To beat any or every opponent or enemy in a competition or fight.
2) To get something as a prize by beating other competitors using skill effort or luck.

The first definition I chose to use in "WIN" fits to a tee. The example is great and I believe every day is a fight or a competition, with you needing to maintain a level of FOCUS to keep you on track. You need to win over yourself in the belief that anything is possible with your PDD, and BOTAAE. What is necessary? If you continue to ask yourself that question and you continue to look for the answer, that internal search will keep you sharp. In order to "WIN" you have to believe you have already won, even before you even get started. Getting yourself psyched up for something happens best when you are prepared for it. Take a look at some of the top athletes in the world or take a look at any extremely successful business professional. Look at how they conduct themselves on every level. In most cases they are extremely humble. They don't have to be flashy or act as if they know everything. The game they play and how they play it, or the way they conduct the business they are in, is how their business becomes successful. Doing, "What Is Necessary" (WIN) to accomplish your goals is how you must look at life. Winning starts in the spirit and your spirit is the essence of your Soul Step, (CONFIDENCE) but it only works if you put in the time and do the work. When I say doing what is necessary, it never means taking shortcuts or breaking the law! For me it is always about the work. Hard work! Being able to see the vision that is your dream has to come into FOCUS. Everything you do starts with a dream. Everything! If you don't believe me ask any person, on any level of what they consider success and you will find they originally had some sort of a dream. Whether they were asleep or awake, they had a dream that always starts in their spirit. Winning with confidence means, "Working hard enough not to fail, but not being afraid to fail."

LIFEWORK JOURNAL ENTRY

I remember there was a period just before I graduated from high school and I was looking for another job. Several of my friends had taken jobs at fast food restaurants and from all the nightmares stories I had heard from them, that was not going to be the job for me. My "DREAM" during that time was to get a job at the Ralph's Grocery Stores in California. I had a good friend, Warren Birdsong who worked for the grocery chain and in California stores like, Ralph's and Vons paid so much better than retail and fast food. They also have one of the best unions in the state of California really taking care of their members. I had a job at another retail establishment at the time, but again my "DREAM" was the get a job at Ralph's Grocery. So, for a little over 7 months, I went into the Ralph's grocery store, at Vernon Ave and Figueroa St. every Monday and Friday without failure. The manager at that time, Andy Small, looked at me one Friday afternoon and said to me, "You really want a job, don't you?" Of course, my response was, "Yes I do Mr. Small" and then he said those magic words… "Be here on Monday at 7AM and you have the job!!!" Needless to say, I was there before Ralph's opened on Monday morning.

END LIFEWORK JOURNAL ENTRY

The second definition of "WIN" is almost as perfect except for the word "LUCK." I said it before, I don't believe in luck. Someone once said to me many years ago that, when it comes to luck he believed, "The harder he worked the luckier he got!" Therefore, hard work is a crucial key to your success, not luck. I don't believe it was luck that I was able to get my job at Ralph's grocery. I don't believe it was luck when I started the testing process for the Sheriff's Department, going through the academy and graduating. I don't believe it was luck how I began working in the world of private security, or working with many of the A-List clients that I have worked with the past thirty years. If you want to call it luck when you are working extremely hard at achieving your goals then be my guest, but I will never call it that. If you look at your FOCUS you have to remember, things happen in your life the way they are supposed to. The way they are supposed to, when you adjust your mindset to the positive and you move your life in that direction. The way they are supposed to when you begin to believe, you belong in the success, standing in front of you! Now because you are aware of the journey you're taking and you are aware of the existence of FOCUS, every person you meet on this journey is placed before you, "FOR YOU!" They are there to help you on your journey. Using knowledge properly will help you learn to allow that "HELP" to happen. Sometimes we need to learn to get out of our own way in order for success to happen.

When I look at no more excuses, I think about how often we make the excuse that everything is so hard, but we refuse to allow anyone to help us. Stop using the "Rebel" excuse, "I have to do it all by myself!" This is one of the easiest ways to set yourself up for failure. "I don't need anybody's help!" Think about how selfish that sounds rolling around inside your brain. We do nothing in this world alone. You know how you get people to help you without even asking? Hard work, it's infectious! Most people that want to succeed at something in life prefer to be with, or work with like-minded people. Pause for just a minute and think about the people you've surrounded yourself with. Are they helping you in any way? Are they helping you to win, or are they helping to create a losing environment. You are the only one who can make that decision, because you created your environment. Help is just a phone call away. Sometimes you will have to ask for a hand or two, or three. This hand or help, from the people who have been placed before you, may offer their help because your FOCUS is showing them you are committed, to whatever you are working on. Either way, your help is here!

BOTAAE is a key component in learning to win. The winning spirit starts in the heart allowing your light to shine brightly throughout our Universe. Darkness can't stop or put out the light. Everybody loves a winner, but most of us don't even understand why. It could be their success or maybe their positive attitude or mindset? Could it be their strength and their courage in times when others would just give up? I have named the attitude or confidence you walk into a room with your "Soul Step." Remember your new way of thinking and living is to do everything outside the box. "No more excuses," is the first part of The Chapter 9 title, but I gave you the "WIN" portion first just so I could influence your state of mind. Influence it in a way that puts excuses in a box locking it away. Let's look at the definitions of excuses.

Excuses is a verb and it is defined as:
1) To release somebody from blame or criticism for a mistake or wrongdoing.
2) To make allowances for somebody or something.
3) Release somebody from an obligation or responsibility.

Excuses could become bad habits and they should never be how you live your life. Just like anything else, excuses can also become a learned behavior. I believe excuses are what you give when you decide to give up. In the definition of excuses, it says, "to release somebody from blame or make allowances for someone or something from an obligation or responsibility." When you allow excuses to rule your life they become a living-dominate factor that assist in you failing. The excuse is "I CAN'T DO THIS OR I'M AFRAID TO TRY THAT!" Fear, which we know will never go away, even though it exists, should not be allowed to rule your world. "FEAR" like anything in your life can only do what you allow it to do as an excuse. You're going to have to learn to control fear by learning to work around it or sometimes pushing through it! I want you to see that you are better than the next excuse you are about to come up with. This is one of those moments you have to let yourself marinate on that last sentence. Everything you are going to do in life has a beginning, middle and an end. Therefore, each component of your life starts and ends with you! You have to be responsible for your actions and you can't look to blame anyone when you don't even try. Excuses! Excuses! Excuses! Stop letting them run your life. Just a little effort is all you need to push excuses aside so that you may become victorious. There is a measure of success inside all of us and it has always been there. Because it's already there, we often ignore it or take it for granted. Sometimes when things come easy to us, the gifts we are given sometimes do not reach their full potential. An idea may come to you that could be worth millions of dollars and it's not about the money, it's about living your dreams. It's about the people that could be helped because of your ideas. Or could it be the fact that, you have something inside you, that won't be satisfied until you get it out of your system and allow it to manifest. Everything begins with a thought…

No one is a born loser. Everything begins with a thought! Losing just like winning, is a learned behavior and in some cases, it becomes an accepted practice, or a way of life. Everything begins with a thought! I have a really good friend, Paul Stephan, and we have worked together on several of the patented products I spoke about earlier. While we were in the development stages of one of our products, a basketball practice shooting aid called, "THE HOOP JAMMER" Paul came up with a catch phrase I decided to incorporate into my life. For many years' people have said "PRACTICE MAKES PERFECT." Paul added to that line, giving it just a little more power and for me he made it Focus Forward by saying, "PERFECT PRACTICE MAKES PERFECT!" This phrase became one of the key bylines to the way I live my life. Everything begins with a thought. We should do everything with the best intentions, but without hard work good intentions are a waste of your time. Having FOCUS will allow you to create that "PERFECT PRACTICE." Over the years I've seen good intention and effort focused in the wrong way because, the "HOMEWORK" was not done. In every case the effort necessary is your hard work in that effort, creating what I call "PERFECT PRACTICE." This is how you destroy excuses!

Everything begins with a thought…

I've learned to use excuses as stepping stones and those stepping stones are there to keep you focused and always pushing forward. Remember, just because you are focused doesn't mean the "N" word won't continue to attack you! It's always going to be there. "WE NEVER GIVE UP!" Newton's Third Law says "For every action there is an equal and opposite reaction." Newton's statement means, that in every interaction, there is a pair of forces acting on the two interacting objects. The size of the force on the first object, equals the size of the force on the second object. The direction of the force on the first object is opposite to the direction of the force on the second object. Forces always come in pairs-equal and opposite action-reaction. This point in Newton's Law for me has to do with every thought or idea you have on the positive side, will always be followed by the

"N" word creeping into those same thoughts attempting to squash them, on the negative side. The larger the thoughts or ideas you have the larger the negative will be! (EQUAL AND OPPOSITE REACTIONS) You may not know or remember this, but we were all born to do great things. Your parents on every level want nothing but the best for you. You as a parent want nothing but the best for your children in everything they do. They want great things out of you. Deep down inside your parents and family want to support you in that success, they really do. I think in many cases, as time passes we lose sight of our goals, our dreams and the visions we have in our spirit. Since we are all born to do great things, when we carry out our intended assignment, the Universe will always benefit. We are all in this together, whether we want to be or not, and we have to understand that everything we do will affect everyone we come into contact with. This is truly where the Yin and Yang are always at work, to keep us in a constant state of balance. I believe the better we do as a group, the better balanced our Universe and environment will become. You help me. I help you… and we all help each other! I know it sounds a little corny, but all I ask is you give it a try and help someone other than you. We may not get the entire world to help each other all at the same time, but what about your immediate environment? None of what we have to do happens overnight. There is no such thing as an overnight success… the hard work was put in years before you knew who that famous person has become. Take a look to your left then your right… the person sitting on either side of you is already putting in the work!

We are human so outside factors are sometimes able to get in and attempt to throw us out of balance. We all experience it, even those with a strong sense of FOCUS lose their balance and sometimes fall, but we do get up and we always get up stronger! One of the best ways to get back on your feet and retain your balance is to stand in front of your mirror and look within to reset your FOCUS. Something I have discovered about myself is, the more focused I am, the quicker I can get back to my mark and my balance is restored. A part of getting your balance and keeping it is, learning that we never give up. Self-evaluation is an amazing tool and it can help you maintain and achieve balance, but you have to be extremely honest with yourself during this process. There is a quote that I have heard for years and never really paid too much attention to, but one day recently it clicked and made complete sense to me: "Nice guys finish last." It's short, sweet, to the point, clear and concise. The revelation that hit me was, "THE GUY FINISHED!" He finished which means he never gave up!

LIFEWORK JOURNAL ENTRY

Several years ago, while in the middle of my daily mirror exercise I had one of the greatest epiphanies of my life. I began to truly understand how and why I never gave up on things. When I decide to do something, the thought is born and fused in my spirit. I understood that this thought was given directly to me. It was mine! Immediately following every thought, the N-word would show up in all of its splendor and glory. I learned to flood my mindset countering the N-word with every reason I could do any and everything that was given to me. "GIVEN TO ME!" I was going to make it work. The quicker I can get the thought to take root in my spirit and grow this allows my Soul Step to be prepared for every challenge, also placed before me. If I stay the course and follow this "THOUGHT" I know I would meet the right people on my journey that would help me accomplish every goal.

END LIFEWORK JOURNAL

No more excuses, you can win has to become a mantra for your life. They say that seeing is believing, so every day you wake up and look in the mirror, you are going to have to believe you "ARE" you "CAN" and that you "HAVE!" Sometimes we don't have the faith necessary to believe without seeing and until your FOCUS has grown to the next level, seeing is okay for now, but you still need to look. Look at what you're doing and look at where you're going, but most of all look at your environment. It's yours, so you have to control it. If I have said it once I've said it a million times, "If you are here on this planet, there has to be a good reason!" Spend a little time each day looking for that reason and don't just go through life walking in circles. Find a direction and move Focus Forward to it. What do you believe the reason is, why you are here? You need to ask yourself that question every day until, you make something happen or you discover your point and purpose. Your search should be never ending!

It's funny, as I look at the plus side of my life even though I grew up in a difficult circumstance, I was told by my parents and several people in my life, I could be anything I wanted to be. The first time I heard those words, I must have buried the essence of each and every word in my "BOX" and they have never failed me. That truly helped me to adjust my mindset early on, even though I didn't think I would live to see thirty years old. I still believed I had a point and purpose, no matter how long or short my life would be, I continued to live my life in a successful manner. I am way past thirty years old and I am truly happy to be alive! I have lived everyday believing in the big picture and as I said before, because the picture can't be completed my goal has always been to continue to work hard at everything I do, every day I live. Early on in Chapter 5 (TIME TO THINK OUTSIDE THE BOX) I asked you to do a Pros and Cons list in respect to your life, and in this list, I wanted you to put these two lists together, examine and evaluate each list and look to the positive side of both. Even in the negative of the cons list, we have to look to find the positive in that and learn from the mistakes, or from a particular situation. I want you to do me favor and take your LIFEWORK JOURNAL and add another chapter to it. This is the "J.O.S." your new assignment is the "JOURNAL OF SUCCESS." The Journal of Success is just that, it's a journal that chronicles successful and positive things that take place in your daily life. You only need one log entry a day to maintain this part of your FOCUS. The J.O.S. will give you a reference point to look to when your FOCUS is challenged. You only need one event per day, but feel free to add as many positive incidents, as you like. A success in your day could be something as simple as slowing down and waiting to open a door for someone, or running an errand for a friend who needs your help. It doesn't have to be anything on a scale of 1 to 10, always being that 10. Your actions will always speak louder than any words. As you write down these small successes it gives you a chance to see what you're doing in your daily existence, to balance our Universe. One of the reasons I want you to do this is, when I was younger and I began power-lifting I kept a journal of my weekly lifting totals and these totals, allowed me to look back and see the successful progression in my lifting, but the journal also allowed me to stay focused on my goals. My goal at the time was to be able to bench-press over 500 pounds. The day before my 30th birthday, I did bench press 505 pounds at Gold's Gym in Venice California. Just because something may seem small to you, that one gesture could be the saving grace in someone's day. Before our minds are reprogrammed to the positive, they have a habit of reliving our negative past, so when you write something in your JOS, it can be quite refreshing to see the positive aspects of our lives on paper. This book, Unlikely Destiny Volume One, is an extremely positive physical aspect of my life. Now that it's out of my spirit and on these pages, I can look at every word, each and every day, because now it lives. It lives out loud in this book. This is one of my journals of success. Think about how many times you let one or two things destroy your day? That incident may have seemed like the end of the world at the time and trust me I have been there, but when I wake up the next day I start my life all over again. It is a new day! When I am blessed enough to wake up in the morning, I can start my positive day all over again. I don't want to ever waste a day. I lost forty-five seconds of my existence! The thought of living my life in a state of negativity, self-doubt, hopelessness, anger, depression, or to just give up, is not why I am here. Greatness calls and I intend to answer. Remember after something happens, you can't take it back; but how you respond to it is what matters. The key to starting a new day, when you get that new day, you can't dwell on what happened the day before. Remember what happened, learn from the incident, but don't let yesterday destroy your life or your FOCUS today, or tomorrow. If you have a chance to do it all over again, your mindset has to be, "Do it better today than you did yesterday!" What are you going to do? Don't keep putting off making a decision on how you're going to live your life. Choose to live it positively.

Tomorrow is not promised to any of us, and since it's not, all the more reason to live your life to the fullest. The JOS is also important to you because the more positive things you can add to your list, you will be able to see your progress and that progress is teaching you to help others. The list you maintain is not a trophy for you to put on your mantle, or on display for the world to see. The JOS is for your eyes only. The JOS will show you that you can do the right thing and it will also show you that success is possible, if you learn to take one step at a time. There is a saying, "Patience is a virtue," so let virtue be your guide in every situation. Hard work PDD and BOTAAE will reign supreme. I want you to understand who you are and let you know that every circumstance you overcome is setting you up for success… not failure! Our lives are a learning experience and we are the living examples of all our experiences. Our successes and failures are the by-product of how we react to what happens in these experiences. The courage we experience in failure, which we pick ourselves up from, is the same courage we show in success. That's what I'm talking about! Who wants to be set up for success? Raise your hand! No really, raise your hand!

In Chapter 1, I mentioned something called Failure to Thrive Syndrome. This syndrome is caused sometimes by defects in major organ systems or problems with the endocrine system, such as a thyroid, hormone deficiency, or other times from abuse and it happens mostly to children and senior citizens. Sometimes when this happens the person's body shuts down causing it to stop growing. It is truly sad when you see anyone, especially a child suffering from failure to thrive syndrome. On the flip side of failure to thrive syndrome, approximately 90% of children who have suffered from this, after being diagnosed, with the proper care and treatment they will completely recover and their bodies begin to grow and develop into full and normal maturity. I'm giving you this example of something extremely drastic to show you a particular circumstance, is not the end of the world. Your present circumstance does not have to become your life's work. More than 90% of these children recover and go on to live normal lives. I want you to understand that you can also recover. You can recover from all of the negativity that had once plagued your life before FOCUS. Now that you're focused you can move forward replacing the negativity with new growth of positive thoughts and an openness to receive BOTAAE the Universe has to offer. If you read your local paper, you will see people all over the world doing things to survive extremely dire circumstances every day, because they choose not to give up. As I open the door to a new path in the history that is my life, I take joy in this new adventure seeing what my life can be, not forgetting what it was, while believing I can… This quote, if you remember was at the beginning of my introduction and it took an enormous amount of thought, but I managed to get it done. I want to let you know I am no different than anyone else. I am a man who believes there is nothing I can't do, if I put my mind to it. Even if I didn't always show it, I truly believed it and you can and will do the same. The strength that drives you to get up and live your life is the same strength that will drive your FOCUS to the positive. I'm not in any way perfect and I've made many, many mistakes, personally and professionally, but I can't and won't stop living my life with a "FOCUS FORWARD" mindset. If you stop, take a look at your life, you will discover you are stronger than you ever imagined and you also know more than you thought you knew. You have met and dealt with challenges you never thought you could endure, or overcome and you did. You have great people in your life and a majority of those people look to the strength you exhibit and because of your strength, they are developing FOCUS. Something I hope you learn is, "Your strength can't be measured by anyone, but it can be felt in ways that would knock the world off its axis." We all have periods in our lives, some longer than others where it seems as though nothing ever goes our way and when this happens, you can develop an attitude of negativity, that begins to take over your entire being. I call this the, "OH WHOA IS ME SYNDROME!" And because of the negative spirit you've developed, you can't see a way out. If this happens you can lose FOCUS and that allows Anger and Depression to set in stealing your Enlightenment. What Is Necessary "WIN" or winning is impossible without you being able to give maximum effort mentally and physically! This journey is yours and yours to complete, but remember there is strength in numbers. Help is right in front of you… you just need to accept it. Every attempt made by someone to help you will be recognized right away. At times it will seem that the help you receive will come from the most unlikely places. By the way… there are no unlikely places when it come to your Destiny. Laying your foundation for success, the people you work with become a major part of your foundation giving you support even when you don't think you need it. As you look to understand what is necessary on your road to success, it might be the road less traveled, but it has been traveled and now it's open to you. While on this road get comfortable and accept the lane you are driving in. If you stay focused and continue with your positive efforts, personal and professional success is sure to follow. Remember, in the success you create through hard work, that success is presented to you, so you are in the position to help others. To create a winning strategy for yourself, you have to look at the life your living and figure what you are missing in that strategy. One of the missing keys in your strategy could be something very simple. Often times the simple things are overlooked because we don't see or think they are a necessary aid in our success. Sometimes it could be just changing your approach to situations ever so slightly. In order to win there are times you may have to bend and bending could be the difference in winning and not being able to achieve success. Even if you find a time in your life that you have to bend in order to move forward, I want you to remember to never compromise your principals, or your dreams just to get ahead. In cases when you have to bend, you do it only to adapt or overcome a particular circumstance(s) that would create obstacles to your success. There will be times when your FOCUS is so strong, you'll be able to roll over or go directly through an obstacle. This could work to your advantage at that time. Patience has to become mandatory in your life. So, if you have to maneuver around something and things take a little longer to gain the positive edge, then keep it moving! I look at the bend as a strategy in the game of football, where the running back uses his speed, quickness, and agility to move around the defensive line of the opposing team. This running back, because of his position in the game, is used to the contact that the game is based on, so he's not afraid of the contact, or the game. As I stated before, fear is present in every thought, idea, dream, or situation you will ever be involved in. This is one of the defenses you must learn to maneuver through on a daily basis. You don't have to be afraid, but why put yourself through the school of hard knocks when you don't have to? He has studied the game, so coupled with his experience and the ninety-five percent God given talent, he was blessed with, the running back has learned to manipulate the game. He's not cheating the system. He has learned to work within the system or bend it in a sense to gain an edge. Here is where that ninety-five percent (PDD) comes into play. Because he chose football and he decided to play running back, he has learned certain skills that have taught him to adapt to what the defensive players would throw at him. I'm a big fan of Le'Veon Bell, the running back for the Pittsburg Steelers. His running style of taking monetary pause, once he reaches the line of scrimmage, to wait and see what the defensive line gives him is amazing. He has the ability to stop on a dime and accelerate past everyone as quickly as stopped. This is the 5% effort needed that Le'Veon Bell, used to increase his running skill set.

I'm using the role of the running back as an example in this story and even though he is blessed with amazing talent and he made the commitment to work in that extra five percent, he still needs the help of his quarterback and the rest of the offense, to accomplish any of his goals. I also want you to look at the team concept and how important help or teammates are in your life. In the vision that you have developed for yourself and the success in that vision is yours to complete. When you look at the football player, like I told you, he's just like you and that ninety-five percent of all that he is, is already embedded in his spirit! That five percent of the effort you find every day to get out of bed, so you can continue to reach for your dreams is always going to be your hard work. It's been said, "good things come in small packages," well this little, tiny, measly five percent known, as "EFFORT" could be the difference between success and failure. Let's look at the definition of effort.

Effort is a noun and it is defined as
1) Mental or physical energy that is exerted in order to achieve a purpose.
2) An attempt to do something especially one that involves a considerable amount of exertion, work, or determination.

The mental and physical energy needed to create effort is completely up to you. When I became a Deputy Sheriff, I made the free will decision to apply and go through the academy and then I had to make the decision to give the ninety-five and five percent effort, to accomplish my goal. Everything begins with a thought and each thought is a goal set and ready to be accomplished. Once you accept an opportunity that has been placed before you, your effort will become the driving force in your life. Your effort creates the ability to open minds, hearts and doors.

There's a definite method to the madness I write with and that madness is to help you create a "Soul Step" that will let your heart breathe freely. There are moments in your life when everything comes together, all of your ducks are in a row and all of the stars have aligned and you are one with the Universe. The effort you find to fulfill your life's vision is also what you need, to help you learn to smile inside. Everybody's idea of success is a little different, so I want you to think about some of the people you share the Universe with, especially those close to you and look at how they measure success. Some measure their success by the number of zeros on their paycheck. Others measure their success by what they do for others. Then there are those who measure their success by the job they worked all of their lives to attain. I have learned over the years that no one is going to agree with what you do one hundred percent of the time, but it is also great to be surrounded by like- minded people. Like minded by having a strong work ethic and believing in their abilities to succeed. There is nothing wrong with how you measure your success as long as you have a goal and do What Is Necessary (WIN) legally and within reason to meet that goal. I believe success should be measured by what you do, with what you have and the work you put in to get it. I told you before, everything starts with a thought, but with that thought action must always follow. For me the thought always comes first, and then I write down every one of them. Then I read them out loud, so I can hear the thoughts. Hearing my thoughts out loud makes them real enough to attain and then I can Focus Forward! Remember thinking outside the box? That's what winning is all about! No more excuses, you can win is what I believe and because I do, my life has changed for the better in every way imaginable, and so will yours. Remember Being Open to Any And Everything? Don't live your life waiting or looking to die! Your life is yours to live so do, "What Is Necessary" to make the best of every moment and live it with no regrets. When you look back at your life, (CLARITY IN MEMORY) you are going to be able to see the moment or the person that helped you in your success. If you thanked them before, call them up, or take them to lunch and thank him or her again! Let them know how they helped to change your life allowing you the opportunity to change other people's lives. Let them know how much you appreciate everything, every moment, every word of encouragement, but most of all let them know what an amazing friend they are to you.

When you learn how to win you will discover that it is truly the gift that keeps on giving! It keeps giving because your success allows you to keep giving! Now that you know excuses can no longer rule your life, by keeping you or bringing you down, you have to know the other side of that is learning to do, "WHAT IS NECESSARY!" Doing "What Is Necessary," in every area of your life, so you can live it with the success that has always been yours. I believe, "Each day is your success waiting to be what you decide to make it." You are a thing of beauty and a joy forever! Let's take a look at the success you are about to encounter...

10

The New Beginning

REVIEW: A QUICK LOOK BACK AT YOUR NEW SUCCESS

Always give your best, never get discouraged, never be petty; always remember others may hate you. Those who hate you don't win unless you hate them. And then you destroy yourself...

Richard M. Nixon

LIFEWORK JOURNAL ENTRY

What a powerful statement in this quote: "Those who hate you don't win unless you hate them and then you destroy yourself..." As I sat down to create the outline for Unlikely Destiny Volume One, I had a little bit of an idea of where I wanted to go and what I wanted to write. Since this is my first book, (IN WHAT I BELIEVE TO BE A LONG LINE OF "UNLIKELY DESTINY" BOOKS TO COME) I had to be truly on point, once I decided to put what was in my spirit on these pages. The outline actually wrote itself and I feel I was able to open the door, to a conversation for living a better life. Once I completed the outline I felt as though Unlikely Destiny also began writing itself. I've had to write in some manner, fashion or form all of my life and I've loved every minute of it. Writing is truly my passion, and my drive. My desire is to wake up each morning, roll out of bed, pray, mirror, and then put pen to paper. "WRITING" is my success every day and I hope you, up to this point have thought about what you consider to be your success. Or I hope what you have read has made you "THINK", even if just for a second. If you have then I've done my job. I have to believe all the writing I've done, has brought me to where I am today, Joe the writer, author of this book and many more to come. Most importantly I have learned the success I speak of, was inside me all the time.

In this chapter: "A Quick Look Back at Your New Success," is just like graduation day. Think about your graduations from Pre-K, Kindergarten, Grade School, Junior High, Senior High, College or even Grad School. These are all truly amazing moments of success, stored in your memory that you will never forget. I mention graduations because they are marquee moments in our lives and everyone has experienced at least one, if not all of these moments. I've told you the memories you create are yours to do with what you will, but you have to review and use them wisely. The more successful memories you can store the more positive examples you'll have to choose from, but don't look past the negative memories. The best thing about a negative memory, is they will teach you what not to accept or put up with! I also spoke earlier in chapter four about quotes and how they help to mark periods in your life, by making these moments special and most of all memorable. The quote at the beginning of this chapter is amazing and I believe it hits home in every area and the true concept of living Focus Forward, "Always give your best, never get discouraged, never be petty; always remember others may hate you. Those who hate you don't win unless you hate them. And then you destroy yourself" By Richard M. Nixon the 37th President of the United States of America. This quote is right on point in every area of the word WIN! What Is Necessary, for you to see the success at being a better person. Success in this quote allows you to see the other people around you, that are necessary to help you balance the Universe we all have to share. This quote is the essence of the yin and yang example, keeping you in line with yourself allowing you to maintain balance, so as not to destroy yourself. My feeling when I read this quote is it could be a guide that has been created to keep you focused. It could also help to keep you grounded, which is a key factor in your development. In my opinion, this quote is close to, or as near perfection, in itself as anything can be. Notice I said, "near perfect." Again, nothing and no one is perfect! I know it sounds crazy, but you don't want perfection. My belief is once you believe you have perfection, you could lose FOCUS, causing you to lose your competitive edge and never accomplish the goals you were put here to achieve. We all have our idea of what we believe is our success every day. "Knowing and understanding what you believe, along with your hard work could aid in making you successful. Believe it or not, the measure of who you are is uploaded into your "DNA" at birth and your life's experiences, bring whom you will one day become, to a medium simmer. It's a medium simmer because we are always learning and ever evolving. Your evolution develops in many cases through time and your life experiences and the environment you create. Even though development is happening you are and should always be a "WORK IN PROGRESS."

When I look at my life there is a quote that comes to mind, that I first heard when I was in the Sheriff's Academy. One of my drill instructors at the time, Sr. Deputy Jim Mahone who was our "Ram Rod," was the person who handed out discipline when we screwed up in the L.A. County Sheriff's Academy. The quote Sr. Deputy Mahone said, was a pick-up line used by many deputies when they get full of themselves, while hanging out at some of the L.A. "Cop Bars" and it goes, "These eyes have seen death a thousand times." Jokingly, this line was used by deputies/cops to pick up women and believe it or not, it works! Not that I have ever used this line, but I do have first-hand knowledge of its use. At the time, it was funny because Deputy Mahone had a way of sometimes making us laugh even when he handed out some of his forms of discipline, but when you think about seeing death a thousand times, that's a little serious. Again, looking at my life from the time I was five years old, I began seeing death and destruction in and around my environment. My first ground zero, when I was five years old, living on 108th street and Avalon street in Watts, California, was where I suffered through the Watts Riots. During that time, (AUGUST 11TH THRU 17TH, 1965) I didn't see or understand the full magnitude of how this event would affect my outlook on how I would perceive life, or even how I decided to live my life. Because I was five years old I didn't fully understand The Watts Riots and I have to believe that was a good thing, but I truly couldn't understand why the people who lived in my neighborhood decided to destroy it. (34 DEATHS, 1,032 INJURED, 3,438 ARRESTED) I do remember how it made my parents and both of my grandmothers feel at the time, because they were extremely sad and at the same time they were very angry about the reason the riots started.

To this day I remember I didn't want to do anything to make my parents angry or sad. I think at that moment the foundation was set and I began to FOCUS on being a better child which made me grow into a better person and on my way to becoming a better man. Looking back as I think about "The Watts Riots," it sounds crazy to me to think about something as devastating as this when I was only five years old. This is when I believe FOCUS was born and began to manifest inside me, growing like a giant Redwood in my spirit, with its roots continuing to grow deeper and deeper until one day it reminded me it was there. I believe FOCUS began my steps to the path I'm on today.

When I look at my first year at, James Foshay Jr. High, (My Second Ground Zero, OCT OF 1973) we experienced several small race riot situations between the Black and Mexican students. There were several situations during and after school where several students were injured from both ethnic clans. I use the word "clans" because that's what we are and we should be proud of our heritage, but not at the expense of hurting or attempting to destroy one another. If we want to continue to exist we have to learn to live together, work together and most importantly grow together, if we want to move Focus Forward successfully. I will continue to say "HUMANS" first. We have to learn that if we destroy one another, we create breaks in our, "Universal Chain" and this break in the chain could be our downfall or it could destroy life, as we know it. Even though another dramatic circumstance took place in and around my life, not realizing what I was doing I kept my nose clean and tried to stay out of trouble. (0 DEATHS, UNKNOWN INJURED, O ARRESTS)

FOCUS has been my guide and as I became more and more directed, my Soul Step grew to a level that helped to develop "ME" and the best part about this is, I had no idea it was happening. I always wondered how the development of my confidence began and during the growth of my confidence, my life would continue to become more positive. As I move forward in my life there are the usual peaks and valleys. There are things going on in and around my life. It's not great, but it is not that bad either. Here we are and its 1992 and I'm working for the Inglewood Police Department. A large bump on my road to date was the 1992 L.A. Riots, after the Rodney King verdict. (APRIL 29TH THRU MAY 4TH 1992) I remember watching the verdict on television and shortly thereafter I would arrive at, My Third Ground Zero. The border between the cities of Inglewood Ca. and Los Angeles Ca. is Florence Ave and Normandie Ave. The collision in this intersection would change my life and the lives of an entire city forever. These Los Angeles Riots would also change the face of law enforcement nationwide. During the L.A. riots one of our main jobs was to stop people from looting, but we also had to pick up and take wounded victims to the hospital. I remember escorting several victims to the hospital that had been beaten during the riots and on one of those trips I saw this man lying on a gurney, in the Daniel Freemen Hospital emergency room. I truly believed he was either dead or very close to it. I later found out the man was Reginald Deny, the truck driver who had been driving down Florence Ave. minding his own business when he was nearly beaten to death by several gang members. My second riot and this situation would last several days… not only for the city of Los Angeles, but for Law Enforcement and for the country. I believe this incident divided our country even further racially, because it became a black and white issue. The white LAPD officers involved in the Rodney King traffic stop and beating sparked the L.A. riots even before the verdict was delivered. During the early 1990's L.A. was a powder keg waiting for the right situation to light the fuse. This was it! My wish is even though our clans are ethnically divided, we are all people, "Human Beings" and one day we will have to make it work or we are going to fail! I hate to use the word "fail", but this is what we will have if we don't wake up. (53 DEATHS, 2,000 PLUS INJURIES, 11,000 ARRESTS)

My fourth Ground Zero and the largest bump on my road of life, was the forty-five second flat-line during my left shoulder surgery. This bump would change my attitude about life forever. This near-death experience allowed me to understand I do have a purpose and a reason for existing in this Universe! This event didn't give me all the answers to every question I have, but it has increased my already veracious appetite for knowledge and it also gave me the ability to see the world in a more focused light. It's given me an understanding of one of life's basic principles: live every day like it's your last and live it with no regrets. Always Focus Forward, always be yourself and most importantly let those you love know you love them! (0 DEATHS, 0 INJURIES, MANY THOUGHTS)

Moving forward, my life has me living in New York. The date is

September 11th, 2001 and terrorists have attacked and destroyed "The World Center Towers." This is my Fifth Ground Zero! I can see the fire of the towers burning from where I live in mid-town Manhattan. Not only do I see the first and second planes hit the towers that day, because I work for the nationally syndicated, "Montel Williams Show," we are on the scene the next day. I am at my fifth ground zero, two-thousand, seven hundred and ninety-seven miles away, more death and destruction. Where is my FOCUS? At this point in my life it is truly helping me. It's my guide, my rock and it helps to control what could have been a very depressing situation. I believe because of everything I saw and endured during 911, if my FOCUS hadn't been directed and I didn't understand we are here to help each other, depression would have been my fate. Fate is a funny thing because we sometimes look at it as the end all to everything and it's not. As a matter of fact, in our society, fate is always used in the negative sense or mostly in respect to relationships. I believe you increase your positive fate by doing and living a positive life. This is how I always see my fate because I choose to. My FOCUS is shaken and never stirred, as it was during a devastating event like 9-11. My focused strength keeps my thoughts always moving in the right direction. Focus Forward has become the sword and shield in my fight to understand the world around me. The reason I say it this way is because, as I said before out of the direst circumstance a Phoenix must rise. I say "must" because we have to get up, dust ourselves off and sometimes start all over again! It is your free will right to do, believe, and live your life any way you see fit. As you review your life, because you are still here lets me know that you never, ever, give up! (2,996 DEATHS, 6,000 NON-FATAL INJURIES, O ARREST AND BILLIONS IN DAMAGES)

It's late in the summer of 2005, August 28th to be exact. It's hurricane season in the gulf coast of the United States, and New Orleans and Mississippi are hit by one of the largest hurricanes in U.S. history, Hurricane Katrina, my Sixth Ground Zero. Because I work for a nationally syndicated talk show, Montel went right into the heart, or should I say, the eye of hurricane Katrina head on and didn't blink. Montel met with every person he could and listened to his or her side, front, back, top and bottom of each story. We flew into the heart of the gulf coast. We did everything we could to help the people in these areas to find a sense of normalcy in these tragic times and bring their true stories to the American people. Montel wanted us to help as many people as possible and he also wanted to deliver positive stories. With all the loss, tragedy and devastation, my FOCUS is as strong as it ever was. I'm finally beginning to understand the purpose of FOCUS and what it does. FOCUS creates clarity when you are unable to see. FOCUS helps you to understand things when you don't think you can. FOCUS is your rock unwavering in the wind and rough waters. FOCUS is the soft voice you hear in a crowded noisy room that cuts like a knife through to your understanding. FOCUS is From Opportunity Comes Unlimited Success and because it is, FOCUS will guide you through the extreme times. FOCUS lets you know once things happen, you can't change them, but you can choose how you react to them. Your reaction will be based on the circumstance you are faced with. BOTAAE helps you in this area so you can see and discern every option placed before you. I've given you a little insight into my FOCUS to show you that no matter how dire the situation is, you need to think outside the box and no matter how hard it maybe you must always look to the positive. I know that sounds crazy right? Look to the positive in a dire situation? Yes, look to the positive! You have one or two choices in life, you can either work hard at making your life better, or you can let the "N" word destroy you by giving into the negative. It will always be your choice, so make sure to choose wisely. (BETWEEN 1,245 TO 1,836 DEATHS, AMOUNT OF INJURIES UNKNOWN, 108 BILLION IN DAMAGES)

You want to hear something utterly amazing? The people I spoke with during my time on the gulf coast showed me something I didn't expect. They were saddened because of their circumstances, but their optimism blew me out of the water. These people lost everything and when I say everything, that's exactly what I mean. Nothing was left in many cases especially for those that lived on the coast, because their homes were literally washed out to sea. In many instances the only thing left was the concrete foundation of what once was a 2-story house. The levies in New Orleans that broke created an unbearable living condition for the families in that area, especially those in the ninth ward. The positive outlook on life that many of the people we encountered had, was amazing to say the least! I am truly learning to live my life and I'm learning to love the life I have. I often wonder why I've been involved in or exposed to these devastating situations during my life thus far "THESE EYES HAVE SEEN DEATH A THOUSAND TIMES." I can't really remember what my emotional state was at five years old, after the Watts riots, but I have to think it did have an effect on my life, because I still hold the memories (CLARITY IN MEMORY). As I said before, if FOCUS was awakened that day, then thank God it was, because it created my Unlikely Destiny! The measurement of my new success could be based on my survival during the tragic circumstances in and around my life. During my law enforcement and personal security careers negative people and situations everyday have surrounded me. I understand it because it comes with the job, but if I had not learned to deal with and control it, I could lose everything including my peace of mind. Remember your success always happens before you survive any tragedy. It's a mindset... "Positive is as positive does." The success happens when you wake up in the morning. Success happens before you go to bed at night. The success happens when you pray and learn to believe in those prayers. Your positive attitude, once you discover it will never leave you. That's success! Open up and free your mind to a new way of thinking, or a new way of looking at your life and begin to live it, like you mean it. When I say, "take a quick look back at your new success," your new success happens every day when you wake up with a "PURPOSE." Don't waste it! When you do what is necessary, success is always sure to follow. Don't give anyone power over you, or your thoughts, and never ever take anything associated with your life, or the lives of those you come in contact with for granted. I will never say, "You may not ever get another first chance," but I want you to always put the best "YOU" Focus Forward every time. It's okay to have your own thoughts and to act on those thoughts accordingly to achieve success. You can be an individual and you can have the space necessary to live your life letting the individual shine, but you won't do anything in this world alone. When I look at sports teams they always say "GREAT PLAYERS" (WHO ARE INDIVIDUALS) make the players around them better! Be that "GREAT PLAYER" and make your family, the people you meet and work with and those who work for you, better! You are only as good as you allow yourself to be or push yourself to be. Success will never be given to you; success is placed before you as everything that happens to you. It's up to you to recognize success just as you would recognize the nose on your face. Go ahead and touch it, or you can just blow it! Your face, your nose, and most of all your success!

Because you have to be open to any and everything in order to envision where you can go, don't be afraid when doors begin to open for you. Having the right FOCUS will create endless possibilities. Appreciate any and all relationships, old and new. I've never really told too many people this, but I try and make it a point to tell people how I feel so they can't say… "You never told me that." I make it a point to do that so I am always comfortable in my skin. One of the worst feelings in the world is not being comfortable with yourself and feeling uneasy around people who you allow to make you feel that way. When you live in a world of distractions, there is no real way to maintain your FOCUS. The way you live or choose to live your life is up to you, but remember to allow yourself to dream and when you dream don't be afraid to live those dreams. Being focused means, being ready all the time to create an environment for success! You should always be the one who tells your life story and as long as you tell the story, free will gives you the choice to make it a story of success. I'm one of those people that truly enjoy a good movie and I love the happy ending, but the best part of every movie is the actual story. I want you to think about your story and how you will get to the end. What steps will you take to create a better story to live a better life? Like I said in the beginning, my hope is that you start to think! Think about everything and when you think you've thought too much, think again. What will be your Unlikely Destiny? Think carefully! Okay one last thing… If dreaming is for dreamers, what are you waiting for? **"DREAM BIG!"**

END LIFEWORK JOURNAL ENTRY

I want to leave you with the following quote…

"I know you're out there… I can feel you now… I know that you're afraid! You're afraid of change. I don't know the future; I didn't come here to tell you how this is going to end. I came here to tell you how it's going to begin. I'm going to hang up this phone and then I'm going to show these people what you don't want them to see. I'm going to show them a world without you. A world without rules and controls, without borders or boundaries, a world where anything is possible… where we go from there is a choice I leave to you". NEO "THE MATRIX"

ABOUT THE AUTHOR

An author, a patented inventor, a dedicated law enforcement officer and a security consultant to high profile celebrities and corporate executives, Joe Pryor has always known how to **"FOCUS"** on translating dreams into reality. Now, he shares his easy common-sense steps, that helped him overcome the odds to find personal and professional success through understanding his **"UNLIKELY DESTINY."** Joe Edmond Pryor Jr. was born on June 7, 1960 as the sixth of eleven children to a Licensed Vocational Nurse that he wouldn't get to know until he was an adult. Instead, he was raised in a lower middle-class home in Watts and Compton California, by his father and step-mother during an unsettled socio-economic and political climate that would change history. After his best friend was killed by gang members, Joe decided to change career-directions and became a Los Angeles Deputy Sheriff, embarking upon a law enforcement career that would span twenty-two years between Los Angeles Sheriff Department and the Inglewood Police Department, with assignments including; Training Officer, Gangs, Narcotics, Weaponless Defense Instructor, Vice, Custody Facilities, and the Superior and Municipal Courts. Joe's calm under pressure demeanor and strategic thinking with quick responses in critical situations, led him to be sought after in the entertainment and corporate sectors for high profile clients such as Montel Williams, Lionel Richie, Teena Marie, Randy Jackson (of the Jackson 5), Blake Lively, Vanessa Williams, Bridget Moynahan, Gerard Butler, Jennifer Hudson, Rachael Ray, Dr. Mehmet Oz, as well as Chris and Mallock Rock, just to name a few.

As Joe's passion to help others grew, a natural part of that progression was manifested in his writing, hence, the birth of his series of books using the theme **"UNLIKELY DESTINY."** The Unlikely Destiny Series uses positive and motivating principals created by Joe to help his audience find their true potential, by understanding **"FOCUS.** It was these universal life principals that captivated people from all walks of life that became the heart of the series. Each time Joe took a positive path in his life, he realized good things happened, causing him to understand that, "From Opportunity Comes Unlimited Success" **(FOCUS)** and with that he understood his Unlikely Destiny would always propel him **"FOCUS FORWARD."** Facing both tragedy and triumph, Joe has translated his experiences into simple rules that now chart the course for his path to success. With each step of Passion, Drive and Desire on his journey, Joe continues to find ways to maintain his focus and now teaches others how to Focus Forward, to achieve their Unlikely Destiny.

CPSIA information can be obtained
at www.ICGtesting.com
Printed in the USA
LVHW09s2143181018
594096LV00001B/91/P